THE COMPLETE BOOK OF
Miniature Roses

OTHER BOOKS BY *Charles Marden Fitch*

Television Educativa (in Spanish)
The Complete Book of Houseplants
The Complete Book of Terrariums
The Complete Book of Houseplants Under Lights

THE COMPLETE BOOK
OF
Miniature
Roses

Charles Marden Fitch

All photographs by the author unless otherwise credited

HAWTHORN BOOKS, INC.
Publishers/NEW YORK

Library of Congress Catalog Card Number: 75-39118
ISBN: 0-8015-1505-X
1 2 3 4 5 6 7 8 9 10

For the plant breeders and hybridizers who bring us
so much beauty through their unique combination
of artistic vision and scientific creativity.

Contents

PART III

Indoor Culture

Acknowledgments

My special thanks to members of the American Rose Society all over the country who so generously offered me their personal notes about miniature roses. Learning how gardeners use and enjoy miniatures around the world has helped me create a book that will provide precise information for everyone.

Hybridizers Lyndon Lyon, Ralph Moore, Harm Saville, Ernest Schwartz, and Ernest Williams were most cooperative in showing me their professional growing techniques and providing specific information about their miniature rose breeding.

Other growers and hybridizers especially generous in sharing experiences and rose plans for the future include Simon Dot Ribas in Spain, John Ewing of West Virginia, Reimer Kordes of W. Kordes' Sons in Germany, Dave Lajoie in Texas, Frances M. Mannell in Kansas, Martin J. Martin of California, Sylvia McCracken in Washington, Sam McGredy in New Zealand, the Meillands of Universal Rose Selections in France, Star Roses in Pennsylvania, Vuyk Van Nes of Holland, and Dr. Cynthia Westcott of New York.

Original photographs are an important part of this book, and I appreciate the enthusiastic help from my photographic assistants Juan Caro, Peter Denenberg, and Christopher Quinn. The photographs in this book were taken on Kodak films with Nikon cameras. Most of the prints were made by the John R. Kennedy Labs.

PART I

ROMANCE
AND
RESULTS

Mini rose 'Baby Darling' begins to bloom while only a few inches tall.

1
Roses in Miniature

Miniature plants have a unique charm found only in a perfect diminutive reproduction of something we are used to seeing much larger. In roses a miniature is not only unusual but also practical. Miniature roses can be tucked into tight places, grown on windowsills, or grouped into collections of a hundred in the space required for a dozen standard-sized rosebushes.

COLORS GALORE

I still meet gardeners who think miniature roses come only in pink or red, and it is fun to show them minis in brilliant orange, stark white, creamy peach, black red, and a variety of forms equal to larger roses. Over the past twenty-five years hybridizers have made such dramatic progress that we now have all the colors found in large roses. Currently hybridizers are providing even more different forms and colors. Already more than 325 miniature roses have been registered and introduced.

SHOWING OFF

Since so many mini roses can be grown in a relatively small garden, thousands of gardeners are trying their skill at growing these delightful flowers for shows. Some regions even have winter shows for miniatures grown indoors under lights when cold weather has put the outdoor garden to sleep.

Even without the challenge of showing roses in competition, a bed of miniatures creates a season-long show in your garden. Beds where stan-

'Peace', the famous hybrid tea rose, towers above a collection of miniature roses including 'Kathy', 'Wee Lass', 'My Valentine', 'Mary Marshall', and 'Starglo', examples of modern miniature hybrids. Airy *Tiarella cordifolia collina* completes the arrangement.

dard roses grow typically have empty space in front of tall canes. Here miniature roses are perfect plants, helping to fill your whole garden with fragrance, color, and a delightful diversity in rose size. Cut all the mini flowers you want because cutting the stems only increases new growth, which in turn provides even more flowers. Miniature roses look delicate, but they are versatile and tough.

OUTSIDE AND INSIDE

You can grow miniature roses indoors during the fall, winter, and spring; cut them back; set the bushes outdoors for the summer; and then begin the process again in the late fall; digging, pruning, potting, finally growing plants inside. To avoid such a seasonal scuttle, follow this plan: Grow miniatures indoors for the winter, enjoy their delightful colors, perfume, delicate beauty. Then when spring comes, put these winter bloomers outdoors permanently. Set them in the garden, toward the front of perennial borders, or in raised beds, window boxes, or separate rose beds, where their beauty will increase each year.

When fall arrives, pot different plants to grow indoors. Every year the hybridizers introduce new selections—exciting color blends, different growth styles, variations on miniature charm. Try these new creations or some older hybrids not yet in your collection. Fall is the perfect season to obtain some new bushes for growing indoors while also gathering the newest charmers for your collection. One warning: after several years of this delightful activity you will be buying more lights for indoor growing and digging up lawn each spring for expanding rose beds. Miniature roses are easy to propagate from cuttings or even from seed.

VERSATILE

Miniature roses complement numerous situations in the garden. A low hedge of 'Baby Masquerade' will provide a tapestry of yellow, peach, cream, and orange all season. Hanging baskets of rich 'Red Cascade' or cool, fresh 'Green Ice' create an unusual display for lamppost, terrace, or front step decoration. Formal beds of minis will furnish countless cut flowers and perfect specimens for show prizes.

Foliage differs among miniature roses. Seen here in actual size are leaves from *(top, left to right)*, 'Kara', 'Tweetie', 'Cinderella'. *Center left*, 'Mimi'; *center*, 'Pompom de Paris'. *Bottom, left to right:* 'Starina', 'Rouletii', and 'Little Girl'.

Two bud forms of miniatures: *left*, the formal 'Mary Marshall'; *right*, few-petaled informal 'Baby Masquerade'

FROM WHENCE THEY CAME

Starting around 1799 and into the 1800s miniature roses were called fairy roses. French and English nursery firms listed several cultivated clones of fairy roses in the early nineteenth century, and the famous botanical artist Mary Lawrance was honored by having the fairy rose type named *Rosa* Lawrenceana. An early report of a cultivated miniature rose is seen in the *Curtis Botanical Magazine* of 1815, where color plate No. 1762 shows a rose labeled *Rosa* Lawrenceana described as *Rosa semperflorens* var. *minima*.

ANCIENT HISTORY

Where the first miniature roses came from is not precisely documented in writing, but botanical evidence traces miniature rose strains back to China. Certainly roses of all types have been cultivated in China for

7

This is the actual page from the 1815 *Curtis Botanical Magazine* showing an early mini rose.

The text published with the drawing presents a description in Latin and interesting comments. (Original book courtesy of New York Botanical Garden Library collection)

thousands of years, and rose flowers are seen in ancient Oriental drawings. Still we have yet to find any miniature rose species growing in the wild.

Taxonomists generally agree that present-day miniatures were derived from cultivated selections grown by seed through many generations. Crossing miniature roses with their own pollen or planting seed from open pollinated flowers gives a range of offspring, with flowers in single to double form, showing colors from white to deep pink.

Such seedlings naturally provide a few select individuals (*clones,* or what we now call *cultivars*) that are then propagated by cuttings or budding, thus increasing the select types through vegetative propagation. Through this system select miniature forms were introduced to Europe by traders who brought plants from the Orient via ports on Mauritius in the Indian Ocean.

PRESENT-DAY MINIATURES

My friend Dr. A. M. Khadaroo of Port Louis, Mauritius, sent me a dried miniature rose that represents a type currently grown in island gardens. Dr. Khadaroo reports that "miniature roses are not grown on a large scale in Mauritius . . . but every garden has some plants." These present-day miniature roses must be direct descendants of roses brought to the island by traders, who often stopped at the Indian Ocean port on their way to Europe from the Orient.

Modern hybrids are derived from a few cultivated miniature types, including one referred to as a species (*Rosa chinensis minima*), although it has not been found in the wild. Another famous cultivar often shown as a species is *Rosa* 'Rouletii'. The original plant of 'Rouletii' was discovered in a Swiss Alpine village, where it was being grown as a pot plant. The history of this rose is well documented in writing, and since *Rosa* 'Rouletii' started the modern miniature on its road to wide popularity, I include the originator's account in full. The first widely publicized mention of this new rose appeared in *The Gardeners' Chronicle* of December 9, 1922, under the heading Foreign Correspondence, where a letter from plantsman Henry Correvon was published. The letter in full reads:

A few years ago a friend of mine, Dr. Roulet, found in a little village near Grandson, a very minute Rose grown in pots in the windows. It was a minuscule shrub, five centimetres high, bushy, and covered with small Roses not exceeding one and a half centimetres broad (just like a sixpenny piece). He told me about the plants and I went to see them; but just at that time the whole village of Mauborget had been

9

burned, so we could not find a single plant. Local people stated that a woman in another village, Onnens, five miles away, had a similar plant. So we went there and my friend obtained a little growth of the Rose, which he gave me. We increased it, and soon had hundreds of plants which I named Rosa Roulettii,* after my friend. This is the most liliputian of all Roses, but where these good people got it from nobody can say.

"It has been grown here for centuries, but only in windows and never out in the garden, as it is too delicate a plant,"—so say the peasants. After studying the subject I found in de Candolle's *Prodromus*, Vol. 2, p. 600, that there was in the beginning of the nineteenth century a form of Rosa indica** II called humilis by Seringe and pumila by Redouté, which is said to be minutis. But mine is minutissima.

In her classical Rose book, Miss Willmott mentions a Rose chinensis var. minima, Rehder (The Fairy Rose), but she means the Lawrance Rose we grow at Floraire, which is not the same as my plant. Who can tell me anything about it? The village of Mauborget, where this tiny Rosa has grown "for centuries," is not far from Champagne, above Grandson, where de Candolle had his garden. Did M. de Candolle grow the plant in his house, and has it been thus distributed in the neighborhood? I could not find any trace of this Rose elsewhere in the country, and nobody, not even old people, could give me any further explanations. They all seem to believe that the minute Rose is an old kind grown from a time immemorial in Mauborget. Of course, it is better for pot culture in windows than in the open ground. We planted some in a bed in order to get material for cuttings, and there it lost something of its character of a dwarf compressed shrub, and grew higher (ten centimetres high). But the flowers and the leaves are never larger than in the case of window plants, and it remains the smallest of all shrubs. It flowers perpetually, and I have just been out to gather little buds from under the snow covering my garden at Floraire, which I send you herewith.

Henry Correvon, Geneva

---

*This account uses two *t*'s for the rose named in honor of Dr. Roulet. However, Henry Correvon in later writings spelled it *Rouletii*, so the spelling in this 1922 letter may be a printer's error.

**Modern horticultural rules always show species names in italics but here I have shown the original style as published in the 1922 letter. Note also that the rose called Lawrance is spelled both with an *a* and an *e* and also as a species name as in Lawrenceana. These minor spelling and style differences occur in the original documents.

This sample of a presently grown miniature rose came to me from the islands where miniatures were first traded many years ago. Now this creamy white miniature would be called a cultivar of *Rosa chinensis minima*.

Fragrant pink 'Rouletii' rose

In this letter of 1922 Henry Correvon mentions several important horticultural attributes of his new rose introduction that are advantages continued in modern miniatures: that the plants are bushy, always have flowers, live through cold winters, and will grow taller if given free run in good garden soil.

Years later, in his book *Floraire: The Genesis and Development of an Old-fashioned Garden* (1936), Henry Correvon wrote personally about his by then well-known discovery:

> We cultivate here and have introduced a Swiss-Italian rosebush which we have distributed in all of Europe and even, with authorization of the United States Government, into the United States. It is a pigmy rosebush which we have described in the horticultural press of France, Switzerland, Germany, Belgium and America under the name of *Rosa rouletii;* after Colonel Roulet of Fontaines sur Grandson, who informed us of it.
>
> This rose has already created a number of interesting discussions and has produced many amusing legends. An American magazine had stated that I had discovered *Rosa rouletii* in the wild state on a crag in the Jura at an altitude of 3000 meters. An elegant French magazine said that it was in Italy on a window of a mountain chalet that I had found the plant, which I vainly tried to buy, the proprietor refusing to sell me even a single branch for rooting; and that finally, having spilled all the gold in my purse on the table, the woman, unable to resist the temptation, gave up the plant.
>
> The facts are much simpler: My friend, Roulet, who lived at the foot of the Jura, above Grandson, informed me one day that he had a potted midget rosebush which grew on a window ledge of a cottage at Mauborget (at 1176 meters altitude); he told me that this rosebush had been grown in this pot for a century, that it bloomed from one end of the summer to the other, that it was absolutely dwarf and belonged to this family for the last 150 years; he offered to give me some branches of it for rooting.
>
> We succeeded in propagating it and, from the very beginning, I realized that this was an interesting variety. That was in 1917, and, from 1920 on, we were in a position to deliver certain quantities. At the present time this plant is on sale at the Flower Market of Paris and large quantities are sold at a high price, ten times as much as we ourselves had sold it. In England, this rosebush has become very popular and the horticulturists have earned for this plant of Floraire the Medal of Honor. It was the same in America where the little Jura

lass is very appreciated. We are dealing with a minuscule everblooming Bengal rose which normally does not grow taller than 10 centimeters, with flesh pink flowers of the size of a five centime Swiss coin, very fragrant and so numerous that, under good conditions, they cover the plant in such a way that they hide the foliage.

My thought on the matter is, as follows; the village which harbored this marvel is above Champagne, where the Grandee of Candolle had his summer property, and where his father retired during the revolution of Geneva. The Candolle described in his *Prodomus* (Vol. II, p. 600) a *Rosa indica var humilis*. Our illustrious botanist was a young amateur at the end of the 18th century, and probably already cultivated interesting plants. Had he Bengal rosebushes of the form *humilis* of which his gardener might have given cuttings to friends and relatives? That is possible and we would thus have the explanation of the origin of this plant.

As far as its miniature dimensions are concerned, it is said that the Japanese produce their dwarfed plants by maintaining them in small pots and poor soil, further reducing their size by very special pruning.

Since our mountain people had kept the plant in the same little pot for an entire century, this may be the explanation of the matter. It goes without saying that many cuttings had multiplied this midget rose, and that the entire village had some, until the fire which destroyed the greater part of the homes. A woman of Onnens, having obtained some cuttings before the fire, was in a position to repeople a number of window ledges of her villages.

It is possible that the lack of nourishment, the fact that the plant has never been repotted, and without doubt also, the meteorological conditions of altitude have contributed to dwarf the plant and to bonsai it. That seems to me much more probable because of the fact that cultivating the bush in fertile soil causes it to immediately lose its characteristic size. In rock crevices or in small pots the *Rosa Rouletii* keeps and even accentuates these characteristics. *

The introduction of 'Rouletii' brought miniature roses to the attention of gardeners around the world. Two nurserymen, Jan de Vink in Holland and Pedro Dot in Spain, began experimenting with hybridizing miniature roses and thus created the first commercially successful modern miniature hybrids. (See chapter 2 for their stories.)

Robert Pyle of the Conard-Pyle/Star Roses Company introduced Jan

* (Geneva, Imprimerie Atar, 1936), pp. 120-121.

Bud grafting is used by commercial growers to obtain more bushes of a new hybrid for testing. A bud is carefully removed from the plant to be propagated.

Step number two is to fit the fresh bud just under the bark of a vigorous rootstock rose, here *Rosa coriifolia froebelii*.

Finally the new bud is held in place firmly, here with a special plastic wrap used at Rosas Dot in Spain. European growers bud graft most of their miniatures, even for garden use, but United States growers propagate miniatures for sale from stem cuttings.

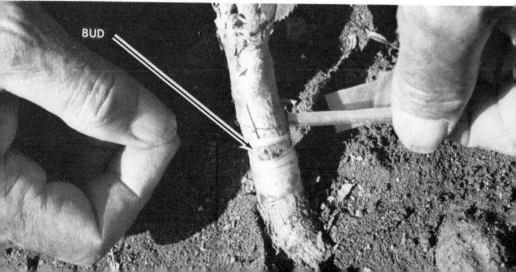

BUD

de Vink's 'Tom Thumb' to United States gardeners in 1936, and it was the first miniature rose to be patented. During World War II Pedro Dot released 'Baby Gold Star' (1940), followed by his still famous 'Perla de Alcanada' (1944) and 'Perla de Montserrat' (1945), thus beginning full-scale hybridizing.

With a greater variety of miniature colors and forms available, the gardening public began to plant more and more of the tiny roses. By the 1950s articles on and photographs of miniature roses appeared frequently in gardening publications. Additional professional rose hybridizers began to work with miniature roses, and the famous firm of Jackson and Perkins joined Star Roses in offering miniatures in their color catalogs. The exciting development of miniature roses continues today at an even greater pace. By blending new species into miniature lines, hybridizers have been able to introduce nearly all of the variations found in standard-sized roses (see chapter 3).

SPECIES IN MINIATURES

Rose characteristics such as fragrance, leaf type, flower color, and form are seen originally in pure species noted for specific desirable traits. By crossing different plants the hybridizer seeks to combine the best traits of each parent into a single new hybrid. This work takes many generations of seedlings and is complicated in roses because some of the so-called species are themselves actually ancient, long-cultivated hybrids.

The genetic background of hybrids causes them to breed in a less predictable fashion than wild species. Fortunately, professional hybridizers learn about their favorite hybrid parents after several seedling generations and are then able to predict the outcome of breeding work with something other than pure speculation.

The species, and old hybrids treated as species, now found in modern miniature roses account for the exciting variation currently occurring with new hybrids. Not all hybridizers are willing to divulge the specific parents of their recent hybrids, especially when commercial contracts are involved. But most of the hybridizers I contacted courteously consented to outline their basic breeding techniques, including the roses used in past and present hybridizing. Those species most prominently used for miniature breeding are:

Rosa acicularis—Through the hybrid 'Therese Bugnet' (*R. acicularis* X *R. rugosa*), this very cold-hardy shrub has been bred into modern miniatures. Lyndon Lyon uses offspring of 'Therese Bugnet' in his new breeding program to get vigor and winter hardiness.

A 2-inch tall blue and gold Limoges vase is filled with flowers from seedlings of *Rosa chinensis minima*. Flowers are all fragrant and range from white to deep pink.

R. chinensis minima—This miniature rose has never been found in the wild. Botanists trace *R. chinensis minima* to China, where it has been cultivated for thousands of years. Hybrids between various forms of this species are in the background of nearly all present-day miniatures. The cultivated roses 'Pompom de Paris' and 'Rouletii' are two presently grown cultivars close to the original. Miniatures sometimes grown as *R. lawran-*

Rosa multiflora nana raised from seed

ceana are botanically *R. chinensis minima* cultivars. Although *R. chinensis minima* is not a pure species found in nature today, it is treated as a species in breeding and international registrations.

R. multiflora—Some miniatures inherit vigor and multiflowered sprays from *Rosa multiflora*, usually through the hybrid polyantha shrub 'Cecile Brunner', an old rose introduced in 1881. For example, miniature 'Cinderella' is 'Cecile Brunner' X 'Tom Thumb' and 'Baby Betsy McCall' is 'Cecile Brunner' X 'Rosy Jewel'; both hybrids show multiflowered sprays characteristic of the multiflora rose species. 'Pink Clouds', a primary hybrid of miniature 'Oakington Ruby' X *R. multiflora* is used at Sequoia Miniature Rose Nursery as understock for their budded mini tree roses. Older books list *R. multiflora* as *R. polyantha*. An interesting strain of *R. multiflora* is offered as *R. multiflora nana* in some seed catalogs, such as Geo. W. Park Company. The seed produces charming bushy mini roses, 8 to 15 inches tall, with clusters of white to deep pink flowers, usually single but some with almost double petals.

Rosa roxburghii, the double pink Chestnut Rose

R. roxburghii—This 4 to 5-foot hardy species from Japan and China was bred into miniatures by Ralph Moore through 'Floradora', a floribunda cross of German hybridizer Math Tantau, made with 'Baby Chateau' X *R. roxburghii.* The species contributes vigor, easy rooting from cuttings, and, through 'Floradora', bright red color.

R. rugosa—This shruby species is originally from Japan but it has naturalized in parts of the Northeast, especially along our coast where it survives salt spray. Through the 5 to 6-foot hybrid 'Therese Bugnet', the *R. rugosa* vigor is being introduced to miniature roses bred by Lyndon Lyon.

R. wichuraiana—This semievergreen but cold-hardy creeper will spread 15 to 20 feet if left unpruned. Clusters of 1½ to 2-inch fragrant white flowers appear during the summer. Hybridizer Ralph Moore has used this Japanese species to obtain adaptability, vigor, and a rambling habit in miniatures. Such rambling hybrids are useful as ground covers and in baskets.

OLD HYBRIDS

Several old rose hybrids appear as key clones in miniature rose history. Besides *R. chinensis minima*, listed above, are its cultivated varieties, such

Left, 'Pompom de Paris', with its rather plain sepals; *right*, 'Rouletii', with its feathery sepals, more open flowers, larger size than 'Pompom de Paris'

as 'Pompom de Paris' (1839) and 'Rouletii' (1917), originally discovered in European gardens.

'Oakington Ruby', found by C. R. Bloom in an old garden of Oakington, near Cambridge, England, was introduced in 1933. Ralph Moore used it for several of his most important foundation crosses. Mr. Moore's lovely 'Yellow Jewel', 'Janna', and 'Windy City' can be traced back to 'Oakington Ruby'.

'Tom Thumb' (syn. 'Peon'), Jan de Vink's first successful hybrid, was created by crossing pink 'Rouletii' with orange polyantha hybrid 'Gloria Mundi' according to de Vink's notes. Red 'Tom Thumb' is still grown, but more important today are hybrids with 'Tom Thumb' in their breeding, such as vigorous 'Baby Masquerade' ('Tom Thumb' X 'Masquerade') by Math Tantau; tiny pink 'Si' ('Perla de Montserrat' X seedling of 'Anny' X 'Tom Thumb') of Pedro Dot; and pink 'Blushing Jewel' ('Dick Koster' sport X 'Tom Thumb') of Dennison Morey.

2
The Dreamers
and Doers

Our modern miniature roses have been created by a small group of imaginative men and women who have hybridized countless roses to reach their dream. Although early hybridizers worked widely separated from one another—in Spain, Holland, the United States—they sometimes used one another's creations to further their own hybridizing goals.

When one worker developed a unique color or form, another breeder might use the breakthrough in an entirely different hybridizing program elsewhere in the world. This exchange of useful genes continues today.

Each year that a hybridizer works, he finds additional breeding clones, those singular plants that are developed within his own program but that may not be introduced because their prime usefulness proves to be in hybridizing. For this reason as the years passed, early hybridizers began to refine their rose lines, doing less and less outcrossing. By using their own stock hybrids for breeding, hybridizers have been better able to predict the outcome of each cross, thus increasing the chances for success.

Still, a hybridizer's work requires much patience and selectivity. Above all, a scientific understanding of genetics is no guarantee that one will create exceptionally lovely roses. A hybridizer must have a creative design, imagination, perseverance, and sometimes pure luck to succeed.

An example of luck occurred when professional hybridizer Ralph Moore created 'Bit o' Sunshine'. Through a combination of accidents Ralph's cross of 'Copper Glow' with 'Zee' resulted in just three seeds. Of these only two germinated. One was the outstanding yellow miniature rose 'Bit o' Sunshine'. Usually hundreds of seedlings must be grown to find one improved form.

Rosebushes at Ralph Moore's Sequoia Nursery carry seedpods with the outstanding miniatures of the future.

THE HYBRIDIZERS

The first modern miniatures were bred by Hollander Jan de Vink, who used pollen from various large roses onto miniature 'Rouletii'. Later Don Pedro Dot of Spain began working with miniatures and soon introduced several hybrids. The Conard-Pyle Company was the first United States rose firm to introduce miniatures. Through their Star Rose catalog the Conard-Pyle Company offered gardeners early miniature hybrids from Europe.

Commercial hybridizers now offering new miniatures in the United States include our first and most prolific miniature rose breeder, Ralph

Moore of Visalia, California. Ernest Williams in Dallas, Texas, is doing some fine work with miniatures, and Harm Saville of Nor'East Miniature Roses in Rowley, Massachusetts, is breeding lovely mini roses.

Some amateur hybridizers are also trying their hand at creating new mini roses but usually without commercial distribution plans. Still other rose growers, with experience largely in different plant families, are accelerating the breeding of miniature roses.

For example, Lyndon Lyon, well known for his unusual gesneriads, is developing his own strain of mini roses. Other hybridizers better known for their larger roses have introduced some miniatures as well. Ernest Schwartz from Maryland created the tiny yellow 'Littlest Angel' and 'Little Linda'. Dr. Dennison H. Morey, formally with the Jackson and Perkins Company, created 'Blushing Jewel' and the outstanding 'Baby Betsy

New miniature bred by Lyndon Lyon is a ½-inch pink (#0-4) that opens to double, long-lasting flowers.

Thousands of new miniatures are tested by the Meilland family in Cannet-Des-Maures, France, where I was photographed in the rose fields looking over future introductions. (Photo by Michel Chauveau)

McCall'. Overseas rose hybridizers who occasionally introduce miniatures include W. Kordes Sons in Germany ('Little Sunset' and 'Bonny'), Math Tantau in Germany ('Baby Masquerade'), G. de Ruiter of Holland ('Crimson Gem'), and Sam McGredy of New Zealand, formerly of Ireland.

Sam McGredy has introduced 'Anytime', a miniature orange red single, and 'Woman's Own', a pink miniature. Of his future plans he tells me that "... my aim would be to produce miniatures in new colors. I am more interested in 'giant miniatures' than in the very small plants. ... Some of the current seedlings of miniature X hand-painted parentage are quite striking." The McGredy "hand-painted" series is seen in his recent floribunda hybrids such as 'Matangi', which feature delicate shadings in contrasting colors, resembling a hand-painted edge. I think we can look forward to some excitingly different semiminiatures from McGredy Roses International in the years to come.

The family of Meilland in France, internationally known for their outstanding hybrid tea 'Peace', has become increasingly active in breeding miniature roses, now introduced by Universal Rose Selections-Meilland.

John Mattock Roses, founded in 1875 at Oxford, England, is world famous for an outstanding catalog of unusual roses. The Mattock firm recently introduced a bushy bright yellow miniature, 'Gold Pin', not yet available in the United States. For the detailed history of modern miniature rose hybridizers we must begin with Jan de Vink, who created the first patented miniature, 'Tom Thumb'.

Jan de Vink

Hollander Jan de Vink was the first commercial nurseryman to have his miniature hybrids widely accepted in the United States of America. Along with early miniatures from Spanish hybridizer Pedro Dot, the de Vink roses were introduced by the Conard-Pyle Company and started the still expanding enthusiasm for these unique plants.

Red miniature 'Tom Thumb' (syn. 'Peon') was de Vink's initial introduction. In 1934 de Vink sent 'Tom Thumb' to Robert Pyle, his new friend, for testing. It became, in 1936, the first patented miniature rose and was introduced in the Conard-Pyle catalog.

Jan de Vink was born and educated in the nursery region of Boskoop, Holland. He was helping bud roses by the time he was ten. He began work with miniature rose breeding in the 1930s, despite the opinions of his friends in Holland, who thought miniature roses had little commercial value; de Vink's tiny treasures were joked about.

Jan de Vink at his nursery in Holland
(Photo courtesy of Vuyk Van Nes)

However, when Robert Pyle, during a European trip in 1933, saw Jan's first hybrids, he realized that with careful commercial distribution there was a future for miniature roses. de Vink's first crosses were with mixed pollen from larger roses onto miniature 'Rouletii'. Although the pollen was mixed from several plants, de Vink identified 'Gloria Mundi', an orange scarlet polyantha hybrid, as the male parent in his first successful miniature, 'Tom Thumb'.

In Jan de Vink's own words he suffered heavy losses in the Great Depression, but when his miniature 'Tom Thumb' got ". . . into the hands of the Conard-Pyle Company, in the United States, the future of this and of my later miniature roses was safe." During World War II de Vink stopped receiving plant royalty money. He had to give up most of his land to cultivation of food crops, and finally was reduced to burning ". . . my garden furniture, my bower, and everything else that we could do without. Then part of my materials in the nursery, and at last my packing shed."

After the hard times de Vink continued his work with miniatures. Eventually he introduced several more hybrids, including the outstanding 'Cinderella', still one of the most charming and widely grown miniature roses. Many de Vink hybrids are still offered by the Conard-Pyle Company in the Star Roses catalog.

The English nursery firm of Thomas Robinson introduced some of de Vink's later miniatures, named after nursery rhyme characters. For example, the Robinson firm released 'Simple Simon' (double pink), 'Willie Winkie' (light rose pink), and 'Humpty Dumpty' (light pink) — all in the

Famous Dutch hybridizer Jan de Vink worked at this small nursery in Holland. (Photo courtesy of Vuyk Van Nes)

1950s. They are charming compact plants but are not widely grown in the United States.

Although forced to work with less than an acre of land, with limited funds, and through periods of great personal hardship, Jan de Vink achieved remarkable results thanks to his vision and tenacity. In 1974 Jan de Vink died, but his creative efforts continue to bring pleasure and joy to gardeners around the world.

Thomas Robinson Nursery

In addition to introducing some of Jan de Vink's miniatures, the Thomas Robinson firm has created several miniatures of their own still found in a few rose gardens. Those most often grown are 'Jack Horner' ('Margo Koster' X 'Tom Thumb'), a round double one-inch flower produced in clusters, a habit inherited from the polyantha 'Margo Koster'; 'Snow White', a 1955 introduction with one-inch double white flowers on a compact shrub; and 'Sunbeam', a fragrant double yellow introduced in 1957.

Pedro Dot

Spanish hybridizer Pedro Dot was born into a horticultural family. His father had a general nursery business and encouraged his son's interest in roses. Soon he had become skilled at breeding new types. In 1927 he introduced the outstanding white shrub rose 'Nevada'.

Starting in the late 1930s, on through the years of World War II, Pedro Dot crossed miniature rose 'Rouletii' with various hybrid tea and polyantha roses. By 1940 his first miniature introduction, 'Baby Gold Star' ('Estrellita de Oro'), was offered in the United States by Star Roses.

Following his initial success with miniatures, Dot continued hybridizing and eventually created more than fifteen unique miniature roses. Many later crosses involved his own early creations as parents. Don Pedro died at ninety-one, in November 1976, but his son, Simon—and his sons as well—carry on Dot Roses.

I visited the Dot rose plantations to study their new hybrids and find out about Dot's method of growing roses. The Rosas Dot farms are located in a fertile agricultural region about thirty miles outside of Barcelona, Spain. The area has rich soil, abundant sun, but a limited rainfall. Dot's rose fields

Simon Dot, son of Don Pedro Dot, looks over a stock of his father's well-known creation 'Sí'.

Sunny, windy, fertile fields of Dot Roses in Spain, where I studied Dot's system of hybridizing miniatures. The rose I'm holding is a famous Dot parent used for producing new hybrids. (Photo by Simon Dot Ribas)

in Vilafranca del Penedes and La Granada, at about 804 feet above sea level, are surrounded by grapes, grown mainly for champagne.

The regional combination of good soil, sun, and irrigation, supplemented with a blend of chemical and organic fertilizer plus a regular spray program help Dot produce outstanding garden roses. Dot concentrates on breeding attractive hybrids for general decoration outdoors.

About 2,000 crosses are made each year. Most of these are for larger roses, but some are to produce semiminiature roses. Simon Dot told me that these are in greater demand than small types. Also, semiminiatures are easier to produce than tiny sorts because buds are larger (Europeans bud graft miniatures) and pollen is more abundant. 'Pilar Dot', a long-lasting coral pink on a 20 to 30-inch bush, is an example of Dot's more recent taller miniatures.

Although Dot's present program is to produce mainly larger roses, you will still find at least 12 of the 24 or so smaller Dot hybrids in current domestic catalogs. In fact, 'Si' is the *smallest* miniature available. Dot roses, like the Meilland hybrids, are introduced in the United States by Star Roses of Conard-Pyle Company. Through commercial licensing arrangements, the Dot roses are sold by other dealers, so you will find Dot's miniatures in all miniature rose catalogs.

Francis Meilland

When Francis Meilland (1912-1958) introduced the beloved hybrid tea 'Peace' in 1942, his rose breeding program became world famous. As a third-generation rose farmer, Francis had an outstanding background to support his imaginative plans. Meilland began to work with miniatures when they first became popular, but not until 1958, the year he died, were his initial miniatures released.

However, the actual crosses for 'Cricri' and 'Colibri', the first Meilland miniatures, were made years before. During a recent visit to the Meilland farms in southern France I observed thousands of new roses and learned the details of their rigorous international evaluation process.

In an average year the Meilland firm makes about 12,000 crosses in search of new garden roses. Crosses made in May or June produce seed by fall. After a 3-week cooling period, seeds are planted. By February the seedlings begin to bloom. The firm, working through Universal Roses, founded by Francis Meilland in 1949, tests promising hybrids all over the world. Initial selection is done by Meilland Roses, with careful supervision

Paper cones protect new seedpods at the Saint André Experimental Estate in Cannet-Des-Maures, France.

Henri Mandoux, hybridizer with Meilland Roses, evaluates miniatures for outstanding characteristics.

Huge greenhouses at Meilland's experimental estate are mounted on rails.

New miniature roses blooming in seedbeds at Meilland's Saint André estate. Stakes indicate those with special promise that will be tested further.

Bud-grafted seedling roses ready for planting out in long testing program of Meilland roses.

Backbreaking bud grafting work is necessary to obtain thousands of plants from a single promising seedling. Here workers graft buds at Universal Roses-Meilland for outdoor testing. The bucket holds budwood.

from Louisette Meilland for miniatures, at the Saint André Experimental Estate in Cannet-Des-Maures, a grape growing region not far from Meilland headquarters, in Cap d' Antibes.

From the 12,000 yearly crosses, made in widely differing directions to increase chances of finding some extra-special plant, about 60,000 seedlings are grown. Part of the 135 cultivated acres at their Cannet-Des-Maures estate is taken up by huge rail-mounted greenhouses, where 20,000 promising seedlings (of the original 60,000) are grown in beds for evaluation their second year. By the third year the greenhouses are slid back on giant rails so that the roses can be grown in the open weather. Bushes are evaluated for shape, vigor, flower bearing potential, cold hardiness, color, and similar important characteristics. Meanwhile the big greenhouses, now over new beds, are ready to receive the next group of seedlings.

European hybridizers such as Meilland and Dot graft roses, even the miniatures, onto rootstocks of *R. coriifolia froebelii* (sometimes called 'Laxa' understock). The grafting is done to increase available wood for further grafting and testing and perhaps eventual introduction. This is in con-

Rail-mounted greenhouses are moved away to let new roses grow in the open after their first year under glass at the Saint André Experimental Estate.

trast to our United States hybridizers, who do all of their miniature propagation by cuttings to produce plants on their own roots.

At Meilland Roses about 1,500 selected hybrids, from the original 60,000 seedlings, are grafted and tested further the fourth and fifth years. Of these 1,500 only 100 are selected for international testing. The 100 hybrids remaining after five years are sent, as budwood for grafts, to be grown in nursery test gardens at Star Roses (Pennsylvania, U.S.A.); Lyon, France; Seville, Spain; and Gulbord, Denmark.

By the seventh year only 30 hybrids remain to be evaluated. Now the bud-grafted plants are tested in many European countries, North and South America, Australia, Japan, New Zealand, and South Africa. Careful study is made of how stable the desirable characteristics are under all these different climates around the world. Conclusive evaluations are done in years seven, eight, and nine.

Finally, after ten years of study and international growing only 2, 3 or 4 of the original 60,000 hybrid seedlings will be introduced. Even then certain hybrids may not be selected for introduction in the United States. All Meilland roses for the United States are introduced by the Conard-Pyle Company. Meilland sends budwood to Star Roses, where the new hybrids are bud grafted to *Rosa multiflora* rootstock. Promising miniatures are later tested as own-root cuttings under garden and greenhouse conditions before Star Roses decides which to offer in their catalog. Unless Conard-Pyle evaluators select a specific variety, they will not be commercially available in the United States because of present licensing contracts.

With such a detailed process of evaluation it is not surprising that between 1958 and 1976 Meilland has given us only a dozen miniature roses. However, among these are the world famous 'Starina'; long-lasting 'Scarlet Gem'; charming pink 'Mimi', so like an old-fashioned rose; and everblooming 'Chipper'.

Careful records show where budwood of potential new releases is sent for testing. This actual page from Meilland records shows budwood sent to the U.S. and six European countries.

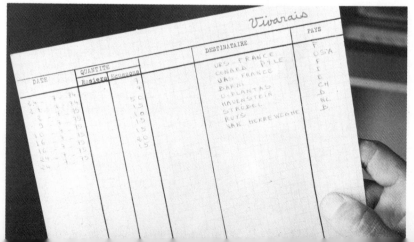

Michel Chauveau of Meilland Roses looks over records of Universal Rose Selections, giving complete evaluations of a new Meilland rose.

A new miniature hybrid waiting for release, growing in fields at Cannet-Des-Maures, France.

Besides the actual miniature introductions, some of Meilland's larger roses form important parents for hybridizers in the United States. For example 'Baccara', a hybrid tea developed as a commercial cut flower, has been imaginatively used by Ralph Moore to breed durable miniatures. Ernest Williams's unique orange yellow 'Gloriglo' has the Meilland 'Peace' in its background. Although Meilland miniatures are not numerous, they are of high quality and unique appearance. Meilland Roses is continuing to do work with miniatures, so we can expect further unique hybrids from France in the years to come.

Ralph Moore

My first view of Ralph Moore's miniature rose plantation was from the air as our jet descended toward Visalia in the San Joaquin valley of southern California. Water to irrigate the fruit and vegetable farms in the sunny dry region flows from nearby high sierra mountains, mainly through underground rivers.

Visalia is famous as the home of Moore Miniature Roses, but other crops are grown in the same rich valley. I saw fields of cotton and olive groves. Timber is harvested in the mountains, and many of Visalia's thirty thousand population now work in new light-industry firms.

Ralph Moore uses almost five acres for his rose breeding work, with several acres taken up by plants in various containers. Large shrub, climbing, and hybrid tea roses for breeding grow with full sun, directly in the ground. Most of the miniature parents are kept in five-gallon cans or big pots.

Thousands of miniature rose cuttings in 2½-inch pots are set on raised benches in full sunlight. Several times each day they are soaked by overhead sprinklers, since Visalia gets but eight inches of rain per year. Newly set cuttings, placed directly in pots of sandy soil, are misted all day long until roots form.

I walked with Mr. Moore through long plastic-covered greenhouses and asked him about the extreme heat inside, at times going over 100°F. He explained that the roses not only grow faster but they do not suffer so long as humidity remains high and air circulation is good. Besides the greenhouses, ground beds of breeding roses, hundreds of feet of raised outdoor benches, and some nearby pomegranate trees with huge fruit, there is an efficient office built of redwood from nearby hills.

Hybridizer Ralph Moore shows
me one of his new seedlings at
the Visalia, California, nursery.
(Photo by Burling Leong)

Visalia, California, Sequoia Nursery of Ralph Moore

Top, miniature 'Small World'; *left,* 'Fire Princess', which is in background of 'Small World', and large hybrid tea 'Baccara' at *right center,* a parent of 'Fire Princess'— all used in Ralph Moore's hybridizing work.

Next door is the shipping room, where roses are pruned and packed prior to being sent all over the world. In one corner is a refrigerator, where seeds of future improved roses have a chilly rest before being planted. Seed planted in January generally produces flowering seedlings by April, at which time Mr. Moore can begin the exacting process of evaluation.

The characteristics looked for in seedlings at their first blooming are base branching, disease resistance, and general miniature form. The actual flower quality is judged at second flowering. Those plants that still look promising at the second flowering are transplanted into 4-inch pots for further study. Finally, if the new hybrid shows continuing superiority, it is grown on in larger 1 to 5-gallon pots for propagating and perhaps breeding. All seedlings not showing promise are selected *out* and composted! Only a few are registered from hundreds of choices.

In the 1940s Ralph Moore began breeding miniature roses, developing his own special seedlings for breeding and selecting only the most

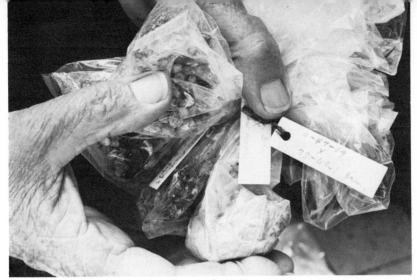

Carefully cleaned and coded seed ready for chilling

Rose seed at Sequoia Nursery is chilled next to the coffee cream, a humble beginning for glamorous new roses.

outstanding clones for introduction. By 1954 he had developed 'Pink Cameo', the first everblooming miniature climber. Soon after came the continuing succession of new miniature forms. Moore's hybrids are now based on over thirty years of custom breeding.

In developing miniature roses, Ralph Moore strives for clones that grow easily, propagate quickly from cuttings, and show different colors, shape, or habit from present hybrids. Although many of Mr. Moore's newest introductions are vigorous 1 to 2-foot bushes with 2-inch flowers, he always takes into account a general miniature style that includes close internodes (compact stems), multiple branching, small foliage, and a generally diminutive bloom, in keeping with miniature standards.

Harm Saville

New Englander Harm Saville of Nor' East Miniature Roses used to be the manager of a dehydrated food plant. As an outdoorsman, he enjoyed occasional on-location projects testing special dried foods designed for campers and hunters, so he has a keen talent for careful evaluative judgment. Saville still works outdoors but now he pours water on rather than supervising its removal. As a hybridizer, Harm Saville must constantly test and evaluate thousands of seedlings each year, always searching for the unusual, the improved.

Saville's rose business began almost by accident. He experimented, first by growing some floribundas indoors under fluorescent lights, in order to have roses during the winter. Then a chance Christmas gift of miniature roses from one of his sons got him interested in the tiny roses. Those six gift plants started a thriving creative business for Harm Saville.

The new hybrids I saw at the eighteen-acre Nor' East rose farm are exciting for their differences. Saville's approach has been to search for unusual colors, particularly intense velvety reds and delicate fragrant pinks. I saw beginnings of a new Saville series that will have rich colors set off by contrasting white centers.

'Pearl Dawn' and 'Little Liza' are early Saville hybrids widely grown indoors and outside. Both are living examples of Harm Saville's skill and imagination. Helping Harm at Nor' East is Mrs. Saville (Chip), who personally grooms each rose they ship. With more than 150,000 bushes shipped each year, that is a lot of loving care!

Hybridizer Harm Saville searches for pollen on new miniature rose parents at his Nor' East Miniature Rose farm in Rowley, Massachusetts.

Harm Saville relates a miniature rose story to me during my research at his greenhouses. (Photo by Christopher Quinn)

Ernest Williams, hybridizer from Texas, shows me one of his special parent roses in the Dallas garden. (Photo by Dave Lajoie)

Ernest Williams

Southerner Ernest Williams hybridizes thousands of roses under the hot sun of Dallas, Texas. Like his contemporary Harm Saville, Ernest Williams began rose hybridizing as a hobby. Only later did the work develop into the commercial venture that has given us such unique hybrids as glowing orange fruit-scented 'Hula Girl' and velvet red 'Miami Holiday'.

Ernest Williams worked for years in creative aspects of printing and photography. After retirement mini rose hybridizing sparked his artistic interests, and now he is again working hard every day, but with roses rather than negatives. Williams explained to me that his goals include breeding for vibrant colors in flowers that show classic hybrid tea form, pleasing perfume, frequent flowering. After growing many of his recent introductions, I know that he is reaching his goals. However in typical hybridizer fashion, Ernest Williams is looking forward several generations. The Williams's busy Dallas garden has hundreds of new crosses being tested. Numerous gems for future years are already sprouting in their redwood flats under the friendly Texas sun.

3
Miniature
Forms

Which miniature roses are best for you? Of primary importance are: What colors do you enjoy? Is fragrance of major or minor importance? Do you wish mainly garden display or perfect show-form flowers? Will you grow the roses indoors or outside?

SELECTION

This book presents a vast array of miniatures together with precise cultural information to help you grow those plants you prefer. However, each rose has specific characteristics that vary somewhat according to culture and climate. A perfect example of a variation in performance is seen in several reports about miniature 'Shooting Star', quoted from the *American Rose Annual* of 1974.

A significant service of the American Rose Society has been the compiling of firsthand performance reports about roses from rose growers in all regions of the United States. These reports are made available as numerical ratings in the annually published booklet *Handbook for Selecting Roses* and also in the form shown below in the society rose annuals. The comments here concern 'Shooting Star', a creation from Meilland in France.

From Ohio the report reads: ". . . a quite showy color in the garden but little else going for it." From North Carolina: "A real good miniature show rose, should go a long way." From New York: "Strictly a decorative miniature, no form to speak of." From South Carolina: "Small bush with a red and yellow blend decorative type bloom, just another miniature." From Minnesota: "Excellent in every way, abundant blooms and can be

'Shooting Star'

exhibition." From California: "This plant is clean, disease resistant and good substance, the blooms high centered and of exhibition quality, a real conversation piece with many blooms."

The reports differ widely for two main reasons: personal preference and different climates, both influenced by cultural practices. The rose society offers a national average rating for miniature roses that is a good indication of garden performance. The reports from various regions are combined to reach a national average, listed on a scale of 10 (perfect) to 5.9 or lower (of questionable value).

As a comparison, the internationally loved 'Peace', a sturdy floriferous, disease resistant hybrid tea, receives a rating of 9.0. Miniatures at or near this high rating include 'Baby Betsy McCall' (8.1), 'Beauty Secret' (9.0), 'Magic Carrousel' (8.6), and 'Starina' (9.4). The booklet that contains the yearly ratings is available for 25 cents from the American Rose Society.

Even better than the national ratings are reports from miniature rose growers in your own state or region. For example, in very cold regions or very warm states the national ratings may suggest cultivars that are in fact not so suitable as similar hybrids that have a lower national average but that thrive under warmer, or survive very cold, conditions. The hybrids I feature in this book have been reported as satisfactory in all regions.

BUSH SIZE

When miniatures first became popular, more than thirty years ago, the available hybrids were quite small. Flowers were less than one inch across, and the shrubs remained 8 or so inches tall with limited pruning. However, the colors to be found in those early hybrids were restricted to pink, white, red, and a few average yellows. When hybridizers began concentrated work with miniatures, several conditions changed: the flowers became more varied in form, available colors increased, various color blends occurred, and bush size expanded. Further breeding has created different forms unknown a few decades ago. For example, we now have mini moss roses, perfect mini climbers, and multipurpose mini roses that respond well to basket culture.

When you choose miniature roses, think about bush size first. There are some hybrids with a 3 to 4-foot spread that have 2-inch flowers, while other selections grow a 6-inch plant with ¼-inch or 2-inch flowers. Both

New Lyndon Lyon hybrid with *Rosa rugosa* in background shows form of this hardy species. This is Lyon #P-16, a bright, long-lasting pink flower.

the catalogs and my descriptions list the basic bush size, but remember that culture also influences the plants' ultimate height.

OLD-FASHIONED STYLES

Some miniatures, although they may be of recent introduction, definitely look like small old-fashioned shrub roses or early rose hybrids as seen in Pierre Joseph Redoute paintings. A few such modern mini hybrids actually have an old-rose fragrance to complement their antique charm.

Regarding fragrance, the introducer of famous miniature 'Rouletii', Henry Correvon, wrote in his book *Floraire:* "If the ultra modern roses in general leave me rather cold, in contrast those of another time speak to me a very interesting language. Among the old beauties of yore the Provence Rose *(Rosa centifolia)* or rose of the King is the perfumed variety par excellence."

'ANGEL DARLING' resembles a *Rosa rugosa* hybrid, but in miniature. The fragrant true-lavender flowers average ten petals each and open to reveal a cluster of attractive yellow anthers. Foliage is glossy, dark green; flowers have an informal undulation. This is a unique Moore introduction, not very beautiful next to reds, but striking planted with a yellow such as 'Golden Angel' or 'Bit o' Sunshine'.

'MEMORY LANE' is a light pink fragrant informal double 1 to 1¼-inch flower produced singly or in small clusters. Nice in window boxes or indoors for the fragrance. Not very vigorous.

'MIMI', a very full double medium-pink hybrid by Meilland, looks like the old-fashioned cabbage roses and has a sweet fragrance too. The parents are a unique Meilland seedling of 'Moulin Rouge' x 'Fashion' crossed with miniature 'Perla de Montserrat', 'Mimi' grows willingly and remains in bloom all winter long on my sunny livingroom windowsill or under lights in the basement. In the garden 'Mimi' will reach almost 2 feet tall if not pruned back; but the long-lived flowers, sometimes darker pink in the center, retain their delicate charm. 'Mimi' is excellent in arrangements.

'POMPOM DE PARIS', with an official 1839 origination date, is the oldest currently available miniature hybrid. In my garden this grows into a bushy 8 to 10-inch tall shrub with few thorns. The fragrant ¾-inch bluish pink flowers are very double and flat centered, 1 to 3 per stem. It is fun to grow for historical interest or to blend with micro yellows and whites in mini bouquets.

'Memory Lane'

'Mimi'

'Simplex' with ripe anthers

'SIMPLEX' is the ultimate in old-fashioned-looking roses because it resembles a pure species such as *R. moschata* or similar single jewels. Buds are apricot but open to single creamy white flowers decorated with a center of yellow anthers that turn dark brown after several days. Indoors under lights I notice that the flowers close up at night, then open in the morning. Freshly cut 'Simplex' does the same, but flowers will last a week in water. Growth is open, with arching multibranched stems reaching 25 inches in a single season. The 1¼-inch, 5-petaled flowers appear in open clusters of 3 to 5 blooms each.

'SPRING SONG' is an older soft-pink informal hybrid from Moore. The 1½ to 1¾-inch flowers are fragrant, long lasting, a lovely spreading plant, perfect in baskets or spacious light gardens.

'WHITE GEM', another hybrid by Meilland in France, is bred from 'Darling Flame' crossed with 'Jack Frost'. The result reminds me of an old-fashioned white rose. The pure white fragrant flowers are very full, heavy substanced, and long lasting, and are produced on a sturdy upright bush

'White Gem'

with dark green shiny foliage. Because of its vigor this is an excellent selection for planting with small perennials or as a bed edging in the garden. Miniature roses bred from the old-fashioned moss rose also remind me of charming cottage gardens.

MOSS MINIS

In 1969 hybridizer Ralph Moore introduced 'Fairy Moss', the first miniature moss rose. This breakthrough was the result of many generations of careful breeding, finally resulting in a cross of a floribunda moss rose ('Pinocchio' X 'William Lobb') crossed with pollen from miniature 'New Penny', another Moore hybrid with fragrant 1½-inch orange red flowers.

Since the introduction of 'Fairy Moss', breeding with moss hybrids has increased. Now at least five outstanding moss hybrids are nationally available, with more on the way. In fact, Ralph Moore told me that one of his major goals is to increase the color range of true miniature moss roses. One new Moore hybrid almost ready for release is a thickly mossed shrub with heavy-substanced rich yellow flowers.

What makes a moss rose special? The fine soft hairs that thickly cover buds and stems look like delicate green moss. At the tip of each mossy hair is an oil gland. The naturally fragrant plant oils from the mossy covering give moss roses a special fresh scent, apart from any flower perfume.

The old-fashioned *Rosa centifolia cristata*, or crested moss rose, has contributed interesting bud crests to modern-day hybrids. Moore has created a shrub or pillar hybrid with cresting on the bud, but with a 5 to 7-foot bush! This hybrid, 'Crested Jewel', also blooms only in the spring. By crossing this sort of new hybrid with true miniatures in various colors, Mr. Moore will eventually obtain short plants that have small delicately crested flowers in constant profusion—but perhaps only after many more years of work. Right now, the mini mosses you will want are:

'DRESDEN DOLL' has mossy buds that first show deep pink, then open into 1½-inch soft shell pink with golden anthers. It is durable in spite of a delicate look.

'FAIRY MOSS' was the first mini moss rose, but it still deserves a featured place in any garden. Buds are heavily mossed, flowers a deep pink, fragrant, often maturing into interesting hips.

'KARA' is a low 6 to 8-inch shrub with slow growth. The 1¼-inch flowers are single, open dark pink, fade to medium pink. Some gardeners report

Mossy covering on 'Paintbrush'

'Fairy Moss'

'Kara'

'Little Liza' growing in a cork pot

'Paintbrush'

that 'Kara' grows in cycles for them. First doing well, producing abundant flowers, then looking sad for a season, and finally doing well again. For me 'Kara' always looks nice, and it does fine indoors under lights too.

'LITTLE LIZA', a recent hybrid from Harm Saville of Nor' East, has 'Fairy Moss' as one parent. 'Little Liza' is a low compact shrub with 10 to 15-petaled deep red pink flowers that open flat and last well. Harm named this hybrid after it had been thrown out into the winter snow as unworthy, then rescued by a customer's young son, who was intrigued by the jewellike plant. The 6 to 8-inch stems are interesting for their mossy covering and are quite compact enough to classify 'Little Liza' as a micro mini, suitable under lights or in rock gardens, where her delicate growth can be appreciated. This gem is difficult to propagate but not hard to grow.

'PAINTBRUSH' is a vigorous Moore hybrid with a very thick covering of light green to golden moss and with fine spines all over the stems and buds. In my garden 'Paintbrush' sends up 2-foot stems topped with clusters of single flowers, opening dark apricot, then maturing to a creamy white. The leaves are a healthy dark green, overall an excellent garden plant. Grow this where late afternoon sun will shine through the mossy stems for an unusually beautiful treat.

FLORIBUNDA STYLES

Miniatures with a floribunda habit make low, bushy growth covered with clusters of flowers throughout the growing season. These shrubs are well suited to edgings, borders, pot culture, window boxes, terrace troughs, and pyramid plantings.

'BABY MASQUERADE', a hybrid from Germany by Math Tantau, is an exceptionally vigorous grower. Stems reach more than 2 feet tall but are bushy and healthy. Flowers open from yellow buds blushed rose, mature into shades of light pink, yellow with red, and blends of these warm colors. Flowers cover the bush from midspring into November. Some mild years I have even had flowers open in December on a plant growing in a protected place. Parents are 'Tom Thumb' and the floribunda 'Masquerade'.

'BLUSHING JEWEL' is one of the original Jewel series created by Dr. Dennison Morey for introduction by the Jackson and Perkins Company in the late 1950s. 'Blushing Jewel' is still worth growing for clusters of 1½-inch pink flowers with almost white centers. The bush is low, 6 to 8 inches, bushy, and quite tough. Parents are a 'Dick Koster' sport X miniature 'Tom Thumb'.

Miniatures 'Baby Gold Star' and 'Nancy Hall' with the large hybrid tea 'Snowfire'

Rosa chinensis minima

An informal bouquet arranged in a demitasse cup

'Small World'

Table arrangement in marble fountain includes 'Pearl Dawn', 'Orange Fire', 'Stacey Sue', 'Little Chief', 'Green Ice', 'Shooting Star', and 'Baby Betsy McCall'

'Beauty Secret'

'Rise 'n' Shine' with heirloom ring

'Littlest Angel' flowers on a four-inch tall bush

'Stars 'n Stripes'

'Miami Holiday'

'Magic Carrousel'

'Starglo'

'Baby Masquerade'

'Blushing Jewel'

'Cinderella' bud opens into a . . .

soft pink pompom. 'Cinderella' is a long-lasting flower.

'CINDERELLA', a de Vink hybrid of 'Cecile Brunner' X 'Tom Thumb', sometimes looks like a micro mini when kept pruned, underfed, or in a small container. However, with rich soil and root room the bush will easily grow to 20 inches in a single spring. Foliage is dense, glossy, and resistant to disease; branching is compact. Although the American Rose Society lists this as white, I seldom see a pure white flower until blooms are several days old. Most open pink, then gradually fade, turning white by the fourth or fifth day. The 1-inch flowers are durable little pompoms, in perfect balance with the small leaves. Outstanding for display, show, and as a cut flower.

'JET TRAIL' sometimes makes a single long-stemmed flower, but once established, stems can reach 24 inches in a few months, then carry clusters of fragrant 1½-inch double white flowers. This Moore hybrid is long lasting both outdoors and cut.

'MY BABY', an introduction from Small World Miniature Roses in Oregon, is the only released mini hybrid from the late Vaughn Quackenbush. I like 'My Baby' for its vigor, its low 6 to 8-inch bushy stems reminiscent of 'Cinderella'—one of the parents—and its clusters of ¾-inch pompom flowers. The color varies from day to day and at times even within a cluster, going from almost white through pink to nearly red, with bunches of 6 to 10 flowers per stem.

ROSA MULTIFLORA NANA is a dwarf strain of the common species multiflora rose so often used as a living fence. Seeds of *R. multiflora nana* germinate easily and soon produce bushy plants with a spring display of single to almost double fragrant flowers, white to dark pink. This is fun to grow but is inferior to modern hybrids in its ability to last and in its blooming season.

'ORANGE FIRE' is a vigorous Moore hybrid with 10 to 15-inch stems and clusters of long-lasting salmon orange flowers. A nice bushy plant outdoors or under lights.

'PLUM COVE' is a recent introduction with 1-inch semidouble plum pink flowers in clusters. The color is vibrant under fluorescent lamps such as Agro-Lites or Gro-Lux. Foliage is small and heavy substanced and the growth is bushy, 8 to 10 inches. 'Plum Cove' is a Harm Saville creation bred from 'Little Chief' crossed with an unnamed seedling.

'POPCORN' is perfectly named for the clusters of ½ to ¾-inch snow white single flowers, each dotted with a bunch of butter yellow anthers. Stems are bushy but can reach 15 inches in a single spring. A unique hybrid with a light fragrance.

'Jet Trail'

'My Baby'

'Orange Fire' growing outdoors with pine needle mulch

'Seabreeze' grown under fluorescent lights

'Stacey Sue'

'SEABREEZE', a lucky creation of hobby hybridizer Marilyn Lemrow, was seen in the originator's garden by commercial grower Harm Saville, who arranged to have 'Seabreeze' formally introduced. The fragrant double pink flowers are different from other miniatures. Sometimes the flowers are almost single, in a very smooth deep pink color, but most of the time flowers are fully double, medium to dark pink, often maturing to almost white. 'Seabreeze' does well for me under lights but in the garden it really shows off, growing 25 to 30-inch multibranched stems topped by clusters of 20 to 30 flowers. Growth is bushy and vigorous, and the long-lasting flowers are produced in true multiflora style.

'SNOW MAGIC', introduced in 1976 by Ralph Moore, is a welcome addition to multiflowered white minis. The 1-inch double flowers come in clusters on 12 to 18-inch stems, looking somewhat like a double version of 'Popcorn'. It was formally known as Moore test rose #78-69-1. 'Snow Magic' looks striking next to red minis.

'STACEY SUE' is described by its originator, Ralph Moore, as looking like "little pink marshmallows." The soft-pink 1-inch flowers are durable, dainty, and abundant. 'Stacey Sue' thrives under lights, where the compact 8-inch stems develop in perfect scale with clusters of tiny buds and blooms.

'Wayside Garnet'

'WAYSIDE GARNET' was offered for years in the famous color catalog of Wayside Gardens and thus is a widely grown mini. The flowers are long lasting, look like a large 'Red Imp', but the variety is actually a sport of 'Oakington Ruby'. The bushy 15 to 20-inch multibranched stems carry clusters of flat-centered ¾ to 1-inch garnet red flowers, which appear very blue toned if seen next to true scarlet flowers.

HYBRID TEA FORMS

A major goal in breeding has been to create tiny duplicates of perfectly formed hybrid tea flowers. This goal has been reached with outstanding miniatures in all the basic colors. The new trend is to retain classic hybrid

Tight, perfectly formed bud of 'Baby
Betsy McCall'

Mature bloom on 'Baby Betsy McCall'

tea form, especially the high-centered flower with tall slow-opening bud, but to add unusual color blends. Today you can plant more than fifty hybrids that show fine hybrid tea form. Some of the best are:

'BABY BETSY McCALL', a Morey hybrid ('Cecile Brunner' X 'Rosy Jewel'), has fragrant light pink flowers. An admirable selection under lights and in bright windows. Stems reach 18 to 20 inches in the garden, with clusters of 3 to 6 1½-inch flowers, a rewarding vigorous yet compact plant.

'BABY GOLD STAR', Dot's formal yellow, can grow to 2 feet in the garden, but buds are perfectly formed. The cut flowers are lovely in arrangements. Light pruning keeps the bush compact.

'BEAUTY SECRET' is a deep red selection with showy fragrant 1½-inch flowers and exquisite slender buds; a favorite at shows. 'Beauty Secret' is vigorous in the garden, where stems reach 20 inches in a season and carry clusters of 3 to 6 flowers. Also thrives indoors under lights.

'BONNY' is a Kordes hybrid in deep pink with ¾-inch buds opening to smooth-finished, long-lasting double flowers. The plant is bushy and has bronze tinted foliage. Elegant.

'CHIPPER', a coral pink hybrid from Meilland, has outstanding vigor and floriferousness, hardly ever being without clusters of flowers from mid-spring into late fall. Flowers begin with hybrid tea form but often appear with 3 or 4 per stem, lasting well, and possessing a light perfume. This makes me think of the new rose division suggested by Jackson and Perkins "Floratea," but in miniature. 'Chipper' mildews easily in my garden, but that does not stop it from flowering for months on end.

'DONNA FAYE' is a recent introduction from Ernest Schwartz, who has been concentrating on creating new miniatures. Parents of this new soft pink are 'Ma Perkins' X 'Baby Betsy McCall'. Flowers on 'Donna Faye' are beautifully formed medium pink show-form blooms with a pleasant perfume. Foliage is medium sized, bushes 12 to 15-inches tall. A fine indoor plant under lights or for garden decoration.

'GLORIGLO', an Ernest Williams hybrid, is a phosphorescent orange with 'Peace' form and ½-inch buds maturing to 1-inch double flowers in glowing orange with a yellow reverse—a unique color combination as the buds develop. 'Gloriglo' blooms on and off all season, always with striking color and smooth texture.

'GOLDEN ANGEL', a Moore hybrid, is a long-lasting yellow with fragrant 2-inch flowers of remarkable substance and depth of color, durable in the garden or as a cut flower. Perhaps the new 'Rise 'n' Shine' has more perfect form, but 'Golden Angel' is still very much worthwhile.

'Beauty Secret'

'Bonny'

'Chipper'

'HULA GIRL' looks like the hybrid tea 'Tropicana', with vibrant orange flowers and a sweet tropical-fruit fragrance. The ¾-inch buds mature to durable 1¼-inch flowers. This Williams hybrid has a distinguished pedigree: the parents are 'Miss Hillcrest', which was bred from 'Peace' X 'Hawaii', crossed with 'Mable Dot', which is an offspring of 'Orient' X 'Perla de Alcanada'.

'JUDY FISCHER', a Moore cross of 'Little Darling' X 'Magic Wand' has fat, ¾-inch buds ½-inch tall, opening into very double formal rose pink flowers. In the garden 'Judy Fischer' sometimes grows an 18 to 24-inch stem with clusters of 4 to 5 flowers; very colorful and long lasting.

'JUNE TIME' is a light pink double with 1½-inch flowers on a vigorous bush. It is lovely planted near a yellow like 'Golden Angel'. It reminds me of 'Stacey Sue', only with a more formal appearance.

'KATHY ROBINSON' is like 'Judy Fischer' in form, but the color is richer, more glowing, with a buff cream reverse. Stems are long, an advantage in showing.

'LAVENDER LACE' is a fragrant true lavender with classic form. This Moore hybrid of 'Ellen Poulsen' X 'Debbie' is the first good mini lavender, a perfect specimen in shows or cut flower displays. This does well under

'Judy Fischer'

'June Time'

'Kathy Robinson'

lights but has the best exhibit in the garden with rich soil. To grow 'Lavender Lace' to perfection indoors, be sure the plant is given a cool rest in early winter. Hybridizer Ralph Moore suggests putting bareroot dormant bushes in the refrigerator for a month, then potting 7 to 9 weeks before flowers are wanted. If plants are wrapped in plastic or roots kept covered with moist sphagnum, they should come through a month in anyone's vegetable bin. (Alternate suggestions for cool rests are found in chapter 9.)

'MAGIC CARROUSEL' wins prizes all over the country for handsomely formed white buds tipped in bright red. The bicolor flower matures at 1¾ to 2-inches across, lasts well both in the garden and cut, and is truly unique. Stems will grow 25 to 30 inches, mainly with single blooms on each stem, but some in clusters of 3. An outstanding rose.

'MARY ADAIR', a Moore hybrid of 'Golden Glow' X 'Zee', has full double apricot flowers from tight pointed buds, nice in shows or the garden. Lightly perfumed.

'MARY MARSHALL' could be classified under floribunda styles. In the garden it frequently sends up 12 to 15-inch stems with clusters of 5 blooms. However, the 1¾-inch coral orange flowers have such perfect form that I list them here. 'Mary Marshall', named after a charming California rose grower, is a superior garden and show plant always ready to put on a display.

'Magic Carrousel'

'Mary Adair'

'NANCY HALL', a peach pink blend, sometimes surprises me by opening a few light pink flowers, a week later going back to apricot peach tones. The 1 to 1½-inch flowers appear freely on neat compact bushes. Nice under lights or in the garden.

'OVER THE RAINBOW' is a red pink blend with yellow reverse petals. It has good form but fast-opening buds. Indoors under lights the yellow reverse matures to white after 3 days. Outdoors this is a vigorous plant.

'PEARL DAWN' has delicate ½-inch light pink buds opening to ¾-inch flowers, 1 to 3 per stem. This Saville hybrid is a true 6 to 8-inch tall miniature bush, in perfect scale with the flowers. 'Pearl Dawn' does well under lights or in the garden. It is small enough to be a micro mini.

'RISE 'N' SHINE', a new golden hybrid from Ralph Moore, has perfect show form. Flowers I cut for indoor arrangements last at least a week. The vigorous bush will reach 12 to 15 inches even in a pot, foliage is large, healthy, in proportion to the 1½ to 2-inch deep yellow, heavy-substanced flowers.

'Mary Marshall'

'Nancy Hall'

'Pearl Dawn'

'SASSY LASSY', a Williams hybrid with brilliant red and chrome yellow buds, opens to fully double, fragrant 1¾-inch red and yellow flowers. Sometimes lots of cream shows in the opening buds, creating an unusual contrast with the vibrant warm colors. Bright and welcome in any garden or show.

'SHERI ANNE', an orange red exhibition-form hybrid of Moore, is bred from 'Little Darling' X 'New Penny'. The ¾-inch tall buds mature to 1¾-inch lightly perfumed flowers that often show a lighter center after several days. This grows well for me under lights and as a garden shrub, growing 18 to 24 inches in a season, with fertile soil.

'STARGLO', a Williams hybrid of 'Little Darling' X 'Jet Trail', has fragrant 1¾-inch creamy flowers, slightly yellow in the center at times, sometimes pure white. Flowers have extreme substance, high centers, and full double petal arrangement. 'Starglo' has great garden vigor and also does well under lights.

'STARINA' is an orange red Meilland creation, world famous for perfect form, it is the most awarded miniature at American Rose Society shows. In the garden I like 'Starina' for intense, long-lasting color. The 1½-inch flowers are slightly fragrant and last well when cut.

'SWEDISH DOLL' is a Moore creation with smooth coral pink flowers looking double in bud but nearly single once fully open. Grows 15 to 18-inch

'Sheri Anne'

Classic bud form of 'Starina'

Open flower of 'Starina'

'Top Secret'

stems, has healthy foliage and good vigor, and lasts well either outside or cut.

'TOP SECRET' is a deep red fragrant sport of 'Beauty Secret' with somewhat more double form, but otherwise very similar. The 1½-inch flowers show clusters of yellow anthers after the third day and are attractive indoors and out. In the garden stems reach 24 inches and terminate in clusters of 5 flowers.

'TOY CLOWN', a Moore hybrid of 'Little Darling' X 'Magic Wand' has won the American Rose Society Gold Medal. The silvery white petals are edged in red and form a double flower 1½ inches across. 'Toy Clown' is vigorous in my garden. It somewhat resembles a small 'Magic Carrousel' but is not as long lasting.

'YELLOW DOLL', a Moore hybrid, has slender buds that open to semi-double clear yellow 1½-inch flowers. This is a favorite in all regions and grows well under lights, too. An unregistered orange mutation of 'Yellow Doll' is 'Maori Doll'.

DIFFERENT DRUMMERS

Not all outstanding miniature roses fit into the perfect hybrid-tea mold. In fact, although the classic long stems, buds, and high-centered flowers may be "ideal," these characteristics are limiting. Many of the most charming floriferous minis dance to a different drummer. Their floral rhythm is expressed with unique form, striking color contrasts, or just plain phenomenal production of flowers.

Many of the minis listed below will be winning rose prizes once judges widen the standards to appreciate new forms. All of these delights will reward you for giving them space.

'Green Diamond' is a vigorous miniature that opens only halfway, first a cream pink, then a light green. Flowers last in perfection for several weeks.

'Crimson Gem'

'ANYTIME', a single orange flower, was bred from miniature 'New Penny' X floribunda 'Elizabeth of Glamis'. Hybridizer Sam McGredy writes me of his creation that it is ". . . a rather ordinary beginning to my work." In my garden 'Anytime' shows vigor and produces sprays of long-lasting flowers that often develop a violet center before fading. Sets hips readily.

'CHRISTINE WEINERT', a Moore hybrid introduced in 1976, grows 15 to 20-inch stems, has clusters of 6 to 8 coral red lightly perfumed flowers. The 1½-inch blooms are very double, last for at least 10 days cut or on the bushy plant, and thrive also under fluorescent lights.

'CRIMSON GEM', a hybrid from deRuiter, is a cross of 'Lillan' with a polyantha seedling. The 1 to 1½-inch double flowers are sturdy, long lasting, and of a very rich color. Although the bush is vigorous, it often suffers from mildew.

'DARLING FLAME', another of Meilland's glowing red orange creations, has 1½-inch double flowers on a vigorous shrub. Mature flowers look only semidouble, show attractive yellow anthers in the center, and set hips frequently. 'Darling Flame' thrives under fluorescents or outside in the garden. Flowers are fragrant.

'DEBBIE' looks like a 1¼-inch 'Peace' rose. The fragrant double flowers are a blend of yellow and pink, presented on a nearly thornless arching stem. 'Debbie' grows well indoors or out.

Fat, round buds of 'Darling Flame' open fast to become fragrant, fertile flowers.

'DON DON', a 1976 Williams introduction, has ultradouble 2-inch flowers with neatly arranged, heavy-substanced dark red petals. Stems are long, the foliage is glossy, and the growth bushy; plants are 12 to 15 inches tall. In my garden this hybrid is somewhat prone to mildew, but the flowers are long lasting, lightly perfumed, and very lovely.

'FIRE PRINCESS' is a Moore cross of red hybrid tea 'Baccara' with miniature pink 'Eleanor'. The result is a 1½ to 2-inch glowing orange red bloom, very durable in the garden or as a cut flower.

'GOLD COIN' is an excellent low-growing garden variety with numerous fast-opening buds, sunny yellow 1½-inch flowers, and small healthy foliage. Parents are 'Golden Glow' X 'Magic Wand'. 'Gold Coin' does well under lights, but the flowers are much shorter lived than more recent yellow hybrids.

'GYPSY JEWEL' was bred by Moore from 'Little Darling' X 'Little Buckaroo'. The medium red flowers are fragrant, double, about 1¾ inches across, buds lighter color on reverse. A welcome hybrid outdoors or inside.

'HUMDINGER' means "a really good one," a perfect description for this recent hybrid. Nor' East Miniature Roses introduced this rose for the 1977

'Fire Princess'

season after having studied its good points for several years. In my garden the bush is dwarf, bushy, vigorous, the thick-petaled double orange pink 1-inch flowers lasting well through rain and sun. The subtle peppery perfume is pleasant indoors. Ernest Schwartz is the creator of 'Humdinger'.

'KATHY', another Moore hybrid, grows multibranched stems with fragrant 1½-inch scarlet flowers, sometimes in clusters of 5, lasting at least 8 days in perfection.

'Gold Coin'

'Kathy'

'Little Sunset'

'LITTLE CURT' has surprising vigor, sending up a yard-tall stem in a few months. Buds are almost black, open into rich blood red 1½-inch flowers, double but opening flat to show stamens. The long stems and durable, long-lasting vibrant flowers make 'Little Curt' perfect as a cut flower—but the bush is not floriferous. This hybrid has the hardest downward-pointing thorns of any mini. Beware.

'LITTLE SUNSET' has 8 to 10-inch branched stems holding a constant display of 1½-inch flowers showing color combinations of orange, yellow, and pink. The flowers last well outdoors or under lights. This is a unique Kordes hybrid.

'MIAMI HOLIDAY', a fine new flower from Ernest Williams, shows bicolor buds smooth yellow outside, dark, intense red within, opening to 1½-inch blooms.

'MY VALENTINE' is outstanding for bushy 15 to 18-inch stems topped with clusters of 1-inch dark red double flowers. I have grown this perfectly under lights, but outside it really shows off, growing a 24-inch stem in a few months. Flowers are long lasting both outside and cut.

'My Valentine'

'Peachy White'

'PEACHY WHITE' was used in breeding by Ralph Moore when it was only seedling #27-62-3. Hybridizer Harm Saville and others liked this so much that plants were sent to test gardens and soon won the A.R.S. Award of Excellence. 'Peachy White' is a quick-opening, nearly single flower, apricot pink at first, maturing to white, sometimes blushed pink. It has done well for me indoors and also makes a vigorous garden bush. (The parents are shown on the chart in chapter 16.)

'PETITE FOLIE' resembles an informal 'Starina'. Flowers are lightly perfumed, a glowing coral orange, with foliage slightly redder than 'Starina'.

'ROSMARIN', a Kordes cross of 'Tom Thumb' X 'Dacapo', earns high praise wherever it is grown. Besides having flowers constantly, the 1½-inch fragrant blooms change in color from light pink when it is cool to darker shades or blends as the weather warms. Growth is bushy and foliage healthy—an outstanding garden hybrid.

'ROSY GEM', a sport of the Meilland 'Scarlet Gem', has starry double pink flowers 1 to 1½ inches across, with petal tips tinted a darker shade. Worth growing for long-lasting flowers that are different from other pinks.

'ROULETII', the miniature used as a parent for many early hybrids, is worth having for historical interest and constant flushes of double pink flowers on 15 to 18-inch stems.

'SHOOTING STAR' has an unusual combination of Indian red and butter yellow heavy-substanced flowers on a compact 10 to 12-inch healthy bush. Color contrast increases with cool weather but is always lovely; flowers are long lasting. (See notes about 'Shooting Star' at the start of this chapter.)

'STAR 'N' STRIPES' will remind you of the old-fashioned Rosa Mundi or *Rosa gallica versicolor* with its white flowers heavily splashed blood red. Moore introduced this delightful miniature for the United States Bicentennial but it will make a perfect Fourth of July bouquet in a blue vase any year. In the garden this grows tall with upright stems to 36 inches.

'TINY WARRIOR', a Williams hybrid, is unlike any other miniature in form. The long-lived 1½-inch dark pink to red flowers are marked yellow inside. Petals form an almost square center and show a delicate filigree vein pattern. 'Tiny Warrior' does well indoors or out. In my garden it resists mildew and blackspot, is very sturdy, compact, and unique.

'WHITE ANGEL' from Moore has creamy white 1½-inch double flowers blushed pink when mature outdoors, though more likely to stay white indoors under lights. 'White Madonna' is similar.

'Tiny Warrior' has square-centered buds.

Open blooms of 'Tiny Warrior' last many days.

'WILLIE MAE' is a long-lasting 1-inch-wide red that makes sprays of 4 to 5 flowers indoors and out. Nice in arrangements with 'White Angel' or 'White Gem'.

'WOMAN'S OWN' is a mini from Irish hybridizer Sam McGredy, who is now working in New Zealand. The medium pink flowers are fragrant and are produced in small clusters on a bush with dark green glossy leaves. The hybridizer reports parents as miniature 'New Penny' X floribunda 'Tip Top'.

'YELLOW JEWEL', an excellent Moore hybrid, makes a bushy plant of deep green healthy foliage and light yellow almost-single flowers of 8 to 10 petals, sometimes marked red in the fall.

'YELLOW MAGIC' is similar to 'Yellow Jewel', but the foliage is darker, with more red tones. It might be pleasing to let 'Yellow Magic' grow into a 15 to 20-inch shrub just for the glossy leaves. These semidouble yellow flowers also blush pink to red when nights are cool.

'Woman's Own'

MICRO MINIS

Now that so many new hybrids have 2-inch flowers and 2 to 3-foot shrubs, I like to group the truly diminutive selections as *micro* minis. The small miniature hybrids are perfect in planters, terrace window boxes, and indoors under lights.

With occasional pruning and moderately rich soil these hybrids will grow into bushy 8 to 10-inch shrubs. Flowers range from the ¼-inch 'Si' to the 1½-inch flowers on 'Scarlet Gem'. If you want these to remain small, then restrict indoor plants by using small containers and pruning. Outdoors apply balanced fertilizer with restraint and prune to make shrubs conform to your plans. Those miniatures most likely to remain small include:

'BABY OPHELIA', a Moore hybrid, grows well in containers, has low full-branching dark glossy leaves and pink and yellow flowers. An unusually attractive plant.

'BO-PEEP', a fully double light pink ¾ to 1-inch informal flower, grows on a low bushy plant. This is a hybrid by Jan de Vink of polyantha 'Cecile Brunner' X miniature 'Tom Thumb'.

'Bo-Peep'

'Little Linda'

'Little Chief' with a few distorted buds on lower spray; flowers quickly returned to normal when watering was increased.

'Red Imp'

'Scarlet Gem'

'LITTLE CHIEF', a Moore micro, has clusters of red double ¾-inch flowers on 6 to 8-inch stems. Multiple flowers form tiny bouquets 3 to 4 inches across.

'LITTLE LINDA' is an exquisitely balanced light yellow with ½-inch buds opening to flat 1-inch flowers. This low, bushy growth is pleasant in light gardens.

'LITTLEST ANGEL', a welcome introduction from Ernest Schwartz, breeder of famous shrub rose 'Sea Foam', is our smallest yellow. The ½-inch butter yellow flowers open to full pompoms on compact, bushy 4 to 6-inch plants. This is a delight in small bonsai pots under lights or in a jewel garden outdoors. Bred from a seedling of 'Gold Coin' X mixed pollen.

'MY BABY' and 'PEARL DAWN', listed elsewhere in this chapter, might also be considered micro minis for their low growth and relatively small flowers.

'PERLA DE MONTSERRAT', an early Dot hybrid, has perfect little hybrid-tea buds opening into medium pink ¾-inch semidouble flowers. This older yet still worthwhile hybrid has been used by modern hybridizers for its perfect bud form and bushy growth.

'PIXIE ROSE', another Dot creation, has dark pink fully double 1¼-inch thin-substanced fragrant flowers.

'RED IMP', a de Vink hybrid, has ½-inch buds opening to ¾-inch dark crimson flowers. Parents are 'Ellen Poulsen' X 'Tom Thumb'.

'ROSY GEM', a rose pink sport of 'Scarlet Gem', is listed previously.

'SCARLET GEM' was bred by Meilland from a seedling of 'Moulin Rouge' X 'Fashion' crossed with a miniature seedling of 'Perla de Montserrat' X 'Perla de Alcanada'. The flower is unique for its rich color and symmetrical form. Plants are vigorous but compact; flowers are long lasting.

'SI', the smallest miniature, has ¼-inch buds that open into ¼ to ½-inch light pink semidouble flowers. Outside stems grow 6 to 8 inches in an average season. 'Si' was bred by Pedro Dot by crossing 'Perla de Montserrat' with a seedling of 'Anny' X 'Tom Thumb'.

'SLEEPY TIME' is a soft peach to salmon pink Moore hybrid bred from 'Ellen Poulsen' X 'Fairy Princess'. I have this bushy mini on a short "bonsai" tree rose stem and find it showy all season long, even in the winter under lights.

'SMALL WORLD' is a deep blood red double with 10 to 15-inch stems and a bushy, multibranched habit. The long-lasting ¾-inch flowers, usually on individual stems, are a delight planted next to a white like 'Popcorn' in a window box.

'STACEY SUE', listed under floribundas, could be considered a micro if kept groomed.

Plant and bud of tiny 'Si'

'Small World'

'Tweetie'

'Perle d'Or', yellow polyantha parent of 'Tweetie'

'SWEET FAIRY' is an older de Vink hybrid bred from 'Tom Thumb' X an unnamed seedling. Flowers are fragrant, appleblossom pink, ¾ to 1-inch across and pompom shape. The plant is low and spreading.

'TEA PARTY' is a restrained grower with 1¼-inch sweetly scented apricot peach flowers. Protect this from root invasion, since it is not too vigorous.

'TINY FLAME' is another low, bushy 6-inch tall shrub that could use more vigor. However the ½ to ¾-inch flowers appear in clusters of 5 to 7 and make a cute show of deep orange pink to almost red.

'TRINKET', a phlox pink hybrid in Moore's micro series, is beautiful for the dark pink, almost red buds. Clusters of 1-inch fragrant flowers make this very special as a mini rose tree. 'Trinket' was bred from a seedling of *R. wichuraiana* X 'Floradora' crossed with 'Magic Wand'.

'TWEETIE', another tiny one from Moore, is an apricot yellow when first open, then matures to pink. Suitable indoors under lights or outside in raised beds, where the well-branched 8 to 12-inch stems will be covered with clusters of ¾-inch flowers. Foliage is light green; the red-toned thorns are not numerous. Parents are 'Perle d'Or' X 'Fairy Princess'.

'WEE LASS' makes a 6 to 9-inch stem, has double tight ¾ to 1-inch medium red flowers.

4
Climbers, Trailers, and Trees

The so-called climbing rose is really a trailing, creeping, or rambling variety with long stems. In contrast to plants that *can* grip their support (ivy, clematis, grapes), roses only produce trailing stems without any holdfast adaptations, such as tendrils.

Some miniature climbers grow 5 to 6-foot stems close to the ground. Such selections are good choices for trailing over walls, hanging in baskets, or even as a ground cover. German hybridizer Reimer Kordes wrote me that ". . . we are looking forward to breeding roses for ground cover."

Another style of climber rose is more upright, eventually arching. Left without special training, such a rose will form a bush of many graceful stems. If these stems are pegged down near the tip, supplementary shoots are encouraged to sprout along the whole cane, each forming a cluster of flowers. 'Red Cascade' is one such hybrid that inherently produces lateral (side) shoots. Moore's 'Happy Time' often does the same.

MULTIPURPOSE HYBRIDS

As a greater number of species are bred into miniature lines and hybridizers outcross with genetically varied parents, the types of miniatures increase. Now you will find miniatures listed in catalogs as "multipurpose" roses. These are robust hybrids suitable as freestanding bushes if restrained by occasional pruning. When permitted to grow at will, however, the plant forms stems long enough for training on an arbor or trellis or for filling a hanging basket or as a ground cover.

Recent examples of multipurpose hybrids are 'Jeanne Lajoie' (pink double) and 'Roseanna' (dark pink double), from Ernest Williams, and 'Red

Climbing miniatures decorate a rustic cedar post support in a Texas front yard. Bush hybrids fill in foreground.

Cascade' and 'Spring Song', from Ralph Moore. After growing many different miniatures I find that some hybrids usually listed as regular bushes will in fact serve as multipurpose roses for baskets, trailing, or arching. The final result depends on the growing conditions and on how you prune.

'Simplex', for example, will remain compact when roots are restrained or soil is not too rich. When roots have a free run in fertile soil, stems lengthen and growth becomes more rapid. However, for the quickest display on walls, arbors, trellises, and in baskets, plant the hybrids specifically recommended as climbers or basket specimens.

TRAINING CLIMBERS

On arbors or other upright supports, gently twine stems around and through the structure as stems grow. Tie the main stem loosely to the wood or metal with plastic garden ties, such as Plas-Ties. Avoid bare wire

'Climbing Pixie' grows with support against a garden wall.

or paper-covered wire. By fastening several sections of stem to the support you will insure against heavy winds or rains pulling down the whole plant. Double-check that the support itself is firmly attached or anchored.

After each flush of flowers cut back stems to conform to your training program. For example, if you wish strictly trained, almost flat espaliered stems, prune back branches to within several inches of the support. If bushy covering growth is your goal, just cut back to the first or second complete leaf (5 or 7 leaflets). Leave late summer stems unpruned for maximum flowering the following spring.

Miniature climbers make a fair display the first summer or fall but really begin a show after becoming established. By the second season you will appreciate how lovely climbers can be.

These are useful plants for covering exterior pipes, ugly foundations, and similar construction details you may wish to conceal. Also consider turning sunny walls into display areas for climbing roses. Even a small garage wall is space enough for 6 to 10 miniature climbers.

WHERE TO PLANT

More than a dozen climbing miniatures are listed in current catalogs. Those that are mutations or sports of regular bush hybrids grow somewhat less quickly than the miniature climbers bred specifically for that use. All of those listed below will grow 3 to 6 feet the first year, then may reach 8 to 10 feet if not pruned in subsequent seasons.

These climbers are suitable for lampposts, garden arbors, and trellises, or to trail over stone walls or grow over big chunks of driftwood. They will also trail well from terrace planters, but be careful that the thorny stems do not grow out into paths. A climbing 'Jeanne Lajoie' in one of my terrace window boxes grew so well that its 4-foot stems blocked a nearby path by mid-August and had to be tied back. Some useful climbers are:

Low bushy miniatures and vigorous climbers provide cover and beauty in front of a foundation.

'Sugar Elf'

'CLIMBING BABY DARLING' is a sport of the fragrant coral pink to apricot Moore hybrid.

'CLIMBING BABY MASQUERADE' is a sport of the vigorous Tantau hybrid, just as satisfactory as the bush. Waves of yellow flowers are decorated with apricot, red, orange, and dark pink.

'CLIMBING CINDERELLA' is a sport of the classic de Vink pink to white double-flowered hybrid. It has glossy foliage and many flowers.

'HAPPY TIME', a multipurpose Moore hybrid with red and yellow 1½-inch flowers, is extra fine once established.

'HI HO', another original climber from Moore, has show-form coral rose double flowers, good both in the garden and cut.

'CLIMBING JACKIE' is a justly famous hybrid with cream to white fragrant flowers in great abundance on a vigorous climber.

'JEANNE LAJOIE', from Ernest Williams, serves well in baskets or trained as a climber. Flowers are double pink with hybrid tea form.

'LITTLE GIRL', from Ralph Moore, has little flowers but long canes. The 1½-inch salmon-blushed coral pink flowers cut well and look good in the garden, too. A good choice in baskets or tied to an upright support.

'PINK CAMEO' is a well-named hybrid with good vigor and a season-long flowering habit. This Moore creation has 1¼-inch double rosy pink flowers in clusters of 3 to 5-foot stems.

'RED CASCADE', from Moore, is an outstanding basket plant, pillar rose, and trailer. The dark double red flowers are long lasting and abundant, thanks to the shrub's habit of producing numerous side shoots from the 4 to 6-foot main stems. This is well suited to training on lampposts or around bird baths, where the flowers show well against a green lawn and blue sky. It is slow to start but vigorous once established.

'ROSEANNA', from Ernest Williams, does fine for me trailing over a rock wall, but it can also be used in baskets or tied to a support. The rich silver pink flowers open to 1½ inches and last well. Parents are 'Little Darling' crossed with an unregistered miniature seedling.

'SUGAR ELF' has pink and gold buds that mature to almost single 10-petaled 1-inch flowers with showy golden anthers filling the center. The glossy leaved bush spreads well and is suitable as a ground cover, in baskets, or in terrace tubs.

'CLIMBING YELLOW DOLL', a Moore introduction, has perfect 'Yellow Doll' double flowers on a sturdy climber. Good in combination with dark 'Red Cascade', either trained together on an upright support or trailing over a rock wall side-by-side.

TREE ROSES

Miniature trees are formed by grafting mini roses onto stems of tall hybrids to create a formal effect. In mild climates mini tree roses require no special care, but where winters are freezing, these tiny trees are not fully cold hardy without protection. However, some mini trees are small enough to bring indoors or bury below frost. In border areas, where winters may be cold but not long or severe, protection with burlap wrap or a similar windshield is adequate.

Uses

Miniature trees provide a display 8 or more inches above the ground. Since tree roses are created by budding miniatures onto a large rose stem, the height can vary. Ralph Moore's Sequoia Miniature Roses offers two sizes of true miniature trees.

'Sleepy Time', a micro mini from Ralph Moore, forms a perfect bonsai-style tree on a 5-inch stem.

In background are 10 to 12-inch stems for trees; in front are shorter, bonsai-style mini rose trees growing at Sequoia Nursery in California.

Grafting miniature buds to taller understock creates a mini rose tree.

The smallest, called a bonsai style, is on a 5-inch stem. I find this size best for growing indoors under lights, in a sunroom or greenhouse. The short stems are in good balance with the miniature flowers and foliage. A container 6 to 8 inches across is quite adequate for the bonsai-style trees, and in such compact pots they are suitable as window box decorations or table displays, and as gifts.

Taller trees are formed by grafting buds onto stems 10 inches above the soil line. Ralph Moore bud grafts all of his tree roses (5 and 10-inch size) on stems of the hybrid 'Pink Clouds', a vigorous cross of 'Oakington Ruby' X *R. multiflora*. In forming the tree a skilled worker inserts the live bud of a miniature just under the bark on top of the understock stem. The photographs show this process.

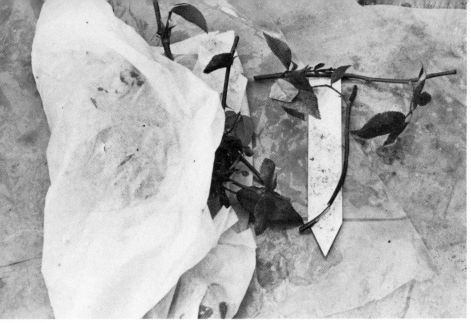

Delicate buds for tree rose grafts are labeled and kept moist during grafting.

The first step in creating a mini tree rose is inserting the bud and binding it with rubber.

After several weeks the grafted bud begins to grow. This mini tree is grafted onto 'Pink Clouds' understock.

Once the top portion is established, the rubber tie is no longer required; the natural rubber will slowly rot away.

Continued Care

A stake is pushed into the soil alongside each tree rose stem, and the bare stem is firmly tied to the stake. If you receive a tree rose without a stake, be sure to supply a sturdy support, such as a stiff bamboo or red-wood pole. Check the tie (plastic-covered wire is suitable) every few months to be sure there is room for stem growth. A healed graft will stand by itself on these stout 'Pink Clouds' stems, but the top growth may get so heavy that it bends over, very likely after a rain. Having a stake always in place protects the stem and makes it simple to maintain an upright, well-groomed tree.

Prune back branches after every flowering. By cutting off each stem tip, at least to the first full leaf, you encourage new branches and frequent flowering. Mini trees need more pruning than the same variety grown on its own root because top growth must be kept in balance with the tall, bare

A miniature bonsai-style tree has part of the rootstock stem above the grafted bud. The top is painted with cane sealer to stop rot.

Ralph Moore trims some of his mini rose trees once the grafted buds are established.

The arrows indicate stems that can be pinched to cause new stems to branch, thus forming a bushy top to this mini tree of 'Sleepy Time'.

'The Fairy' is a semiminiature polyantha shrub, often grown as a tree rose. I grew this specimen one summer on a bright terrace.

stem. If the stem happens to send up a shoot from ground level or along the usually bare stem, twist it off, since this is an unusual sprout from the understock root.

Selections

The smaller hybrids, such as the micro minis, look most graceful as short trees on 5-inch stems. For indoor growing or in small containers outside, the micro minis budded onto 5 to 10-inch stems are most practical.

Outdoors, in garden beds or terrace troughs, any size miniature, from tiny 'Si' on a 5-inch stem to the so-called miniature 'The Fairy' on a 2-foot

'Cinderella' can be trained as a tree by careful pruning. This miniature tree is not a graft but a single bush of 'Cinderella' trained as a standard by John Ewing.

stem, will do. Pick hybrid size and stem height to complement your planting design. Give the nursery a season's advance notice if you have special requests. Not all miniature hybrids are offered as trees, even though any can be bud grafted onto tall stems.

Among those true miniatures currently listed as trees on 10 to 12-inch stems are: 'Beauty Secret', 'Fire Princess', and 'Starina', in the red tones; 'June Time' and 'Judy Fischer', in the pinks; 'Baby Gold Star', 'Bit o'Sunshine', and 'Golden Angel', in the yellows; and 'Jeanie Williams', 'Baby Darling', and 'Toy Clown', in the multicolored blends.

Listed on short bonsai-style stems are such small-flowered sorts as 'Trinket', 'Cinderella', 'Red Imp', and 'Sleepy Time'. The short 5 to 10-inch mini rose trees are offered mainly by Ralph Moore's Sequoia Nursery at Visalia, California, but may sometimes be found in other miniature rose catalogs. These small trees can be ordered by mail just like the regular mini rosebushes.

'The Fairy' with its 2-inch pink flowers in clusters makes an attractive patio or sunroom specimen when grown on a stem of 'Dr. Huey'. (Photo courtesy of Geo. J. Ball Co.)

LARGER TREES

The wholesale nursery of Geo. J. Ball Company grafts patio tree roses onto 20-inch stems of 'Dr. Huey', an old large-flowered climber that provides sturdy understock. The patio trees with miniature roses on top are Moore hybrids. They are sold wholesale to garden centers and nurserymen around the country. You can obtain them by ordering through a large garden center in your neighborhood.

A tree before pruning

The same tree after branches have been thinned and shortened. New flowers will begin in several weeks.

Already popular, after being nationally available at garden centers for several years, are patio trees of 'The Fairy', a pink semiminiature polyantha hybrid of great vigor and cold hardiness. The true miniature patio roses should become just as popular once they are widely distributed. Those types generally offered in the 20-inch patio trees include: 'Golden Angel', 'Kathy' (scarlet), 'Magic Carrousel' (white and red), and 'Red Cascade'.

Winter Care of Patio Trees

Since the patio roses are much larger than the small 5 to 10-inch trees, they cannot usually be moved indoors with ease and thus require special care outdoors where winters go below 10° for any length of time. For optimum protection the stems should be gently bent down and covered with about one foot of soil. The time to do this is just before the ground is frozen and all growth on the tree top has stopped.

If the top stem will not bend down far enough, you may have to dig up part of the roots to make the tree lie flat. Be sure to recover all the roots and water them well before covering the whole plant with more earth. Top the earth mound with salt hay or straw (see drawing in Chapter 9). This protection stays on until the ground fully thaws in the spring.

MINIS IN BASKETS

Long-stemmed and trailing miniature roses can form a bushy bower of bloom when grown in hanging baskets. New hybrids such as 'Green Ice' and 'Red Cascade' perform perfectly in hanging baskets either indoors, in a greenhouse, or most popularly outdoors during warm months.

'Green Ice' as a basket plant

Keeping the plants moist is no problem if you fill the basket with a soil mixture that contains a hydrogel amendment. My experience with Viterra, a hydrogel from Union Carbide, has been rewarding. By mixing 2 to 3 cups of hydrogel Viterra powder into each bushel of potting soil I can cut watering chores by more than half. The hydrogel holds moisture within the soil until roots require water. A hydrogel mix may go 4 to 5 days without water, while the same basic soil mixture without hydrogel might have to be watered every day or two.

Suitable Containers

Another success factor for basket minis is to pot them in plastic containers that do not transpire water. Traditional clay or wood baskets permit water to evaporate through the sides, but most plastics prevent this. Naturally, in a very wet or humid climate you might not need plastic baskets; but most of us have to contend with dry winds and sunny summers. Under these conditions it is an advantage to use a container that does not contribute to water loss.

Contemporary plastic and polyethylene baskets are offered in 8 to 12-inch sizes, well suited to mini roses. You can choose from different colors and decorative styles, but keep in mind that too fancy a container will distract from the roses.

Some superior hanging containers offered nationally include the foam polyethylene Jiffy Hanging Tubs, sold with a three-position brass chain. The black tubs look like cast iron, but the Jiffy tubs come in green and white as well. Drill or burn drainage holes into any hanging container that does not already have them.

Another sturdy national brand is Plexite, with a new line of baskets that have clip-on saucers and a nylon cord for hanging. Sizes range from 6¼ inches to 10¼ inches. The larger containers are best for roses outdoors, where small pots dry out quickly.

Redwood baskets are beautiful with roses. To help these expensive wood baskets last longer and preserve moisture for the roots, line them with heavy plastic stapled to the inside just out of view at the top. Cut a few holes in the bottom to insure good drainage. Keeping the damp soil away from direct contact with the wood will add years to the life of wooden and cork containers. (See photos of window box construction in chapter 7.)

Larger sizes of cork planters are useful and attractive, but like redwood, they are expensive compared to plastics. The cork planters from Portugal

Holes can be drilled in cork planters to create favorable growing conditions for roses.

usually have resin-coated waterproof bottoms of wood fiber with no drainage holes.

If used for direct planting, drill several holes through the resin-coated base. Since these cork pots do not have hangers, they are best suspended with one of the clear plastic pot hangers that supports a container with four almost invisible plastic monofilament lines, such as the Hang-Up device, available in several different lengths.

Hangers and Hooks

Outdoors it is vitally important to hang baskets on strongly fastened hooks. Planted plastic or redwood baskets weigh 15 to 20 pounds, clay and ceramic versions even more. Hooks to hold these weights must be hard metal such as black iron, or sturdy brass hangers designed as outdoor fixtures. The fragile dime store bird cage hangers may do for smaller indoor plants, but outside with a heavy basket of roses they can easily snap, twist, or bend.

The new plastic baskets usually come with galvanized wire hangers or strong nylon hanging rope. On top will be a loop or half-moon hook. These fit onto whatever hanger you have on the wall or overhang. For baskets to hang from a roof overhang, hooks deeply set into a beam are suitable supports.

The fancy net or macrame hangers designed to hold a pot are really not appropriate for roses. The thorny branches get tangled in the net and even miniature roses need so large a container outside that by summer's end the total volume and weight are more than these fabric or rope hangers should hold.

Several devices are offered to hold pots by supporting the container on a small bottom plate fastened to an adjustable length of cord or clear monofilament line. One of the least conspicuous, designed to hold about 20 to 25 pounds maximum weight, is called the Hang-Up, available in 24, 36, and 48-inch lengths.

The only thing weak about this device is the tiny ½-inch hook provided with it. But you can put the clear plastic Hang-Up ring over something sturdier or buy a more practical screw-in hook that goes at least 1 inch into sound wood.

Selections for Baskets

Outstanding as basket roses are 'Red Cascade' and 'Green Ice'. Both of these modern minis form naturally long bushy stems with many upright clusters of flowers, although only 'Red Cascade' is labeled a climber. With a minimum of pruning these selections will form a good basket display.

Plant 3 or 4 small plants in each 10 to 12-inch basket. The size of the plants shipped by mini rose specialists will form fine baskets if you put at least 3 bushes together in the larger baskets. A single plant will eventually fill a basket, but you may have to wait two seasons for that to occur.

In addition to 'Red Cascade' (deep red double with 1-inch flowers) and 'Green Ice' (double opening white, turns pink, fades to green), you should try some of the climbers. Pinch stems to obtain bushy growth on the climbing selections.

'Judy Fischer', the fragrant hybrid-tea-style mini, is so willing to grow and bloom that I have used her in baskets with good results. The rich pink looks good interplanted with cool 'Green Ice'. Commercial grower Harm Saville at Nor' East Miniature Roses plants baskets each spring and agrees that 'Red Cascade' and 'Green Ice' are the best choices for baskets. Other

Fragrant pink 'Spring Song' as a basket plant

excellent hybrids are 'Sugar Elf', 'Pink Mandy', and 'Spring Song'. One of my most successful miniature rose baskets was planted with unnamed minis grown from seed.

Seedlings

As an experiment I planted a sturdy Lockwood 10-inch plastic basket with seedlings of *R. chinensis minima*. The mix used contained hydrogel to retain moisture. By August the basket was full, creating a fragrant display in white, pink, and dark rose. Seedlings of *R. chinensis minima* are exceptionally fragrant and easy to grow. Seed for these come from European seedsmen via the Geo. W. Park Seed Company. Several of the roses I grew from seed are equal to some of the recent named hybrids, but flowers are open to pompom types, not hybrid tea form. All easily form clusters of interesting hips, but cut these off to keep bushes flowering in summer. Leave them on after late fall flowers fade if you want some nice orange berries for winter display.

PART II

OUTDOOR CULTURE

5
Sun and Soil

Roses thrive with bright sun. Plant your miniatures where they will receive maximum light. Some of my roses get only 4 hours of direct morning sun and they bloom adequately, but bushes with longer direct exposure produce more flowers and sturdier stems. If you currently grow good standard roses, feel free to plant miniatures in the same situation. Sunny beds are ideal for roses, and 6 hours of direct sun will produce perfect results.

Light midday shade cast by nearby trees is an advantage in regions with low humidity or summer heat waves. Broiling sun fades some flowers, especially if humidity is low. Subtle apricots and bicolors such as 'Magic Carrousel' may look best with some shade in regions with very hot summers. However, in most parts of the world full sun is best for miniature roses.

With strong light, abundant water, and fertile soil your mini roses will produce prize blooms in quantities sufficient for cutting and garden decoration as well. As shade increases, the floral show will gradually decrease until finally the mini roses in deep shade hardly bloom at all.

Sometimes a newly prepared bed will be perfect for several years, then gradually the bushes will produce fewer flowers and growth will be weaker. This is usually due to branches from nearby trees casting more shade each year. I solve this problem by removing lower branches on the big trees, a process sometimes called raising a tree. Pruning out lower branches may actually improve the appearance of your specimen trees by revealing attractive bark and inner shape. High dappled shade is better tolerated by roses than dense shadows from close-by branches.

Roses grow best in soil that contains a high percentage of humus (rotted organic matter). Of course drainage is important, but most gardens are well enough drained to promote good root growth on miniatures. Just avoid planting minis where the soil stays soggy.

I like to include rough sphagnum peat moss and perlite to improve soil structure. The peat moss helps retain water, and the perlite lightens the soil, helping roots to grow.

BEDS OR HOLES

If you are using miniatures to complement established garden plants, you will want to prepare a single hole according to my line drawing. Fill the hole with well-prepared soil formulated by mixing garden earth with equal parts of perlite and coarse sphagnum peat. Add vermiculite if you live in a region that suffers long rainless periods or if drainage is ultrasharp.

When an entire section of garden is to be prepared for roses it is better to dig up the whole bed and mix in the ingredients throughout the planting sections. First spade the soil to a depth of 1 to 2 feet and break up all lumps, then sprinkle gypsum on clay soils.

In areas where the natural soil is heavy clay the gypsum will improve soil texture and also furnish useful calcium needed for healthy cell functioning.

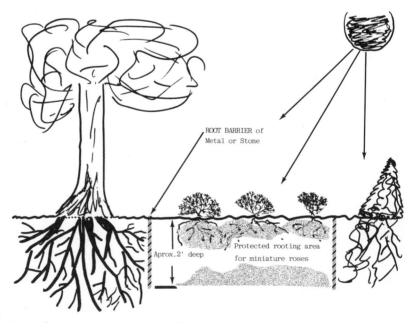

A root barrier of metal or stone will protect a mini rose bed from invading roots. Low branches of nearby trees are pruned to permit sunlight free entrance.

I began a terraced rose bed for new miniatures by outlining the basic shape with large fieldstones partially sunken into the earth. A sprinkling of dolomite limestone and gypsum was sprinkled on the soil, then dug in along with peat moss, perlite, and vermiculite.

The second step for this new miniature rose home was to create informal multi-levels with slate and redwood, both later to be hidden by bushy roses. I took this photo in April. By mid-June the whole area was a sea of miniature rose branches and blooms.

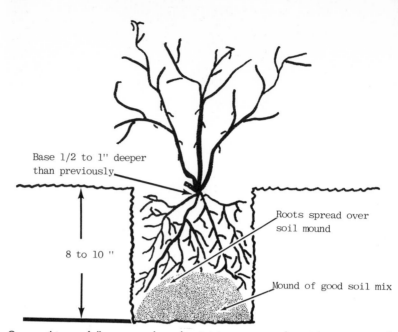

Base 1/2 to 1" deeper than previously

8 to 10 "

Roots spread over soil mound

Mound of good soil mix

Once soil is carefully prepared, each miniature rose can be set in a generous hole with roots surrounded by an ideal mixture.

Gypsum (calcium sulfate) as supplied for horticultural use is a fine white powder, somewhat like dolomite limestone, but gypsum alters soil texture without changing the acid/alkaline balance (pH).

Broadcast 15 to 20 pounds of agricultural gypsum over every 100 square feet of rose growing area. Dig in the powder to loosen heavy clay soils at the same time as you are mixing in the peat moss and other soil additives.

If the soil is very acid (pH 5.0 or less), add agricultural dolomite limestone at about 5 pounds per 100 square feet of soil surface to obtain a pH of between 5.6 and 6.5.

Miniatures grow in a wide range of soil types from acid 5.5 pH to neutral 7.0 pH. In too acid or too alkaline soil the plants cannot make efficient use of available nutrients. Therefore, additional fertilizer is not a complete solution to improper pH. A slightly acid soil promotes the best growth (5.6 to 6.5).

Inexpensive soil testing kits will give you a general idea of how acid your soil is. If you are already growing good standard roses, you can forget about soil testing because the same soil conditions will grow excellent miniatures.

Raised beds are easy to construct with cement patio blocks. The bed will be filled with a specially prepared rose soil.

ALKALINE REGIONS

In some of our southwestern states and in southern California, soil and water are both quite alkaline. Yellow and multicolored miniatures are somewhat less able to produce true-colored flowers than red flowered roses.

Miniature rose specialist Ralph Moore recommends that gardeners in alkaline regions add extra drainage under roses. One efficient way is to make raised beds with 6 inches of gravel and stones under at least 2 feet of especially prepared soil. Mix the best possible local loam with 50 percent rough peat moss by volume. Also add about 25 percent vermiculite.

Mix in 2 to 3 pounds of iron sulfate or ½ pound of ground sulfur per 100 square feet of soil surface. Once bushes are growing, use an acid-balanced fertilizer. Fertilizers offered for azaleas and camellias are acid balanced and in alkaline regions will help you grow better mini roses.

These steps will help you grow sturdy roses in all color classes, even though your water may be very hard and the local soil alkaline. Contact local agricultural agents or one of the nearby consulting rosarians of the American Rose Society for precise advice directly tailored to your garden soil conditions. The American Rose Society will send you the names of the consulting rosarians in your neighborhood.

GENERAL PREPARATION

Aside from the correct acid/alkaline balance, soil structure should be loose, well drained, and slightly on the heavy side. Soil prepared carefully before planting will save lots of future labor and help greatly in growing superior roses. Even heavy clay soil will produce excellent roses if you modify it correctly.

Prepare garden soil by mixing it with humus, coarse peat moss, vermiculite, and perhaps some of the other conditioners listed below, according to your soil. Dig in the ingredients thoroughly, then permit the bed to settle for a week before planting. To be sure settling occurs, even if it does not rain, water down the newly prepared bed after work is finished.

SOIL AMENDMENTS

Which materials you use to improve soil depends on the basic soil type in your garden. If you are currently having success with larger roses or other garden plants, you can begin with miniatures in confidence that they will thrive.

However, if you are a beginning gardener preparing soil in a new garden at a recently constructed home or in a region where you have not had a

Limited protection from invading shrub roots can be provided by small barriers sunken around the planting area of each miniature rose—a practical method where mini roses are planted among assorted garden plants.

garden before, contact a nearby consulting rosarian for friendly free advice on soil preparation.

Most soils will be improved by the addition of coarse peat moss, 25 to 50 percent by volume. Where soils are already slightly acid, as in regions where one finds many oak trees, mix powdered dolomite limestone into soil when using peat moss. Useful soil amendments and their basic functions are:

BARK: Ground bark acts like a cross between humus and peat moss. For the first year, before it decomposes, bark keeps the soil from packing and helps the earth to absorb heavy rains. As the bark rots, it adds humus to the soil and increases its water holding capacity. In parts of the Southwest such as Texas, where soil and water are very alkaline, some rose growers routinely mix redwood bark with the soil to help keep it loose and acid.

DOLOMITE LIMESTONE: This dry granulated powder resembles finely granulated sugar. It is a slow acting, nonburning lime perfectly suited for general garden application.

A big wheelbarrow is useful for mixing soil ingredients. Here, good topsoil is mixed with perlite, rough peat moss, vermiculite, and a dusting of dolomite limestone powder.

125

GYPSUM: Gypsum powder acts as a catalyst in the soil, improving clay by chemically altering molecular structure.

HUMUS: Rotted organic materials—generally leaves, twigs, and compost—improve the soil by adding some nutrients and loosening heavy clay. In sandy soils the humus helps retain moisture. A good rose soil mix is equal parts of humus, sand, and clay.

PEAT MOSS: Coarse sphagnum peat moss is useful for increasing water holding capacity, lightening heavy soils, and acidifying alkaline soils. Fine black peat is not as long lasting, so I prefer coarse sphagnum as the most efficient type.

PERLITE: This is a lightweight white volcanic rock, available in several grinds. Coarse and medium grinds are suitable for lightening soils. Perlite holds water and air, encourages good roots, does not pack, and lasts for years. Perlite is made from volcanic rock heated to 1,700°F. to expand particles to about 13 times their original size.

VERMICULITE: Heating mica rock to 1,400°F. until it expands creates the vermiculite used horticulturally. Terra-Lite is a nationally offered brand of high quality vermiculite, now also seen as the base for ready-to-use Terra-Lite Rose Bush Planting Soil. Vermiculite lightens soil, holds water in its layers, and absorbs water-soluble salts. Roots can draw on fertilizer absorbed by vermiculite, but the mica layers also act as a buffer against over-fertilizing.

6
Water, Fertilizer, and Mulch

WATER

Water must be supplied during the entire growing season for mini roses to reach their maximum beauty. Less than sufficient water will cause plants to lose foliage and have small flowers; and if drastically deprived, the bushes will die. If your roses receive a natural rain of about 1 inch per week, you will not have to water with a hose. When there is less than an inch of rain per week, begin to soak the soil around each bush.

A soaking of 4 gallons per square yard is sufficient if the rose bed has been prepared as recommended. Very sandy soils will need more, while quite heavy soils require somewhat less. Established roses in well-drained beds will accept at least 2 inches of water per week and grow better for it. If drainage is good and the weather is sunny, you need not worry about letting the hose or soaker run slowly overnight to drench the soil.

A slow steady stream of water from a hose soaker or bubbler is a useful method of drenching the soil around your miniatures. The Gurgling waterer and Dramm water breaker devices are nationally available brands that break the force of hose water but let a great quantity pour out. If bushes are some distance from each other, use one of the multiple-tip hose attachments such as the Soakeze. This green vinyl and brass device screws onto a standard garden hose, thus converting the single stream of water into six smaller streams. Each hose branch is 4 to 12 feet long. Another useful product for thorough watering is a soaker hose, made from tough canvas or perforated plastic. The water slowly percolates from the hose, sinking into the ground without wetting the rose foliage.

A rain gauge set in a bed of miniature roses shows total inches of rain or overhead water received by the plants.

Complete Soaking

It is important to soak the earth completely when watering. If you only wet the top inch of soil, the bushes will soon grow a shallow network of roots just below the surface. These shallow roots are quite susceptible to heat and drought injury, even under a mulch. That is why soil must be soaked to a depth of 10 to 12 inches.

This complete soaking encourages a deep, healthy root system, more apt to survive prolonged droughts. Even though you may plan to water regularly, there may be times when it is impossible, such as during a vacation trip or when your municipality has a water restriction. If the bushes have a deep root system, they will come through a temporary drought with little more than some top growth loss.

Watering Systems

Watering devices come in a bewildering assortment of styles, but each design is actually suited to a specific situation. The overhead watering devices are fine for lawns but somewhat risky for roses where black-spot fungus is a problem, because water spreads the fungus spores. On the other hand, overhead watering is useful for keeping spider mites under control. The important point is to be sure foliage has a chance to dry before dark.

Overhead watering done early in the morning seldom causes black-spot problems and will help discourage the mites. A low pattern, three-way sprinkler or swinging lawn sprinkler will do a good job of spreading water evenly.

Ground watering discourages fungus problems by preventing the easy spread of spores. Rose flowers are also protected from possible water damage. The canvas soil soakers are excellent for drenching soil without washing away mulch.

I also like the six-tube Soakeze device because this lets me place water directly at the base of various roses, even though they may be planted among other plants or in odd places on terraced grounds. All of these various devices are found in the larger local garden centers and in the mail order catalog of Mellinger as well as from some of the other firms listed in chapter 19 source lists.

FERTILIZER

Miniatures, like larger roses, flower most abundantly on new growth. When bushes have adequate water and sun, fertilizer will increase flower production. A balanced formula, containing nitrogen, phosphorus, and potassium (potash) in almost equal proportions, works well over most of the country. Rarely, specific deficiencies may occur for gardens in isolated regions or micro climates. Contact a local agricultural agent if nationally available fertilizers do not give satisfactory results when used as directed. Local soil conditions may require an unusual nutrient ratio or trace element.

Slow-Release Fertilizers

Slow-release fertilizers are very convenient. Apply the recommended quantity of these plastic-coated granules around each shrub, and fertilizer will be supplied for 3 to 6 months. Each brand has slightly different application rates, but all will give good results if used as directed on adequately watered plants.

Water is required to release nutrients from the coated granules, and the release is slower with low temperatures and reduced moisture. This means that slow-release fertilizers are well tuned to the needs of growing roses, because when plants are dormant and do not require fertilizer, the slow-release products are also "dormant." Some slow-release product directions suggest that the fertilizer be mixed into the soil; but they work in a similar fashion, releasing the maximum nutrients with abundant moisture and warmth.

Foliar Feeding

Fertilizing roses by spraying a nutrient solution on the foliage is fast and effective. Foliar feeding is an excellent supplement for bushes otherwise fed by slow-release products. I add weak fertilizer to every fungicide or insecticide spray. Well-nourished plants are better able to resist disease and insect damage. Excellent foliar fertilizers include highly soluble Miracle Gro and Peters. When iron chlorosis is a problem, add to the fertilizer spray an iron chelate such as the Geigy Sequestrene 330 in a ratio of 2 tablespoons per gallon of water.

Dry Fertilizer

Standard garden fertilizer, such as 5-10-10, applied dry around each bush is satisfactory but is more work to apply during the season than the slow-release products, which are spread but once. However, you can safely spread a dry fertilizer before early spring growth, then also apply a slow-release product just as the first flowering occurs.

Where winters are freezing, apply no fertilizer after mid-August. The exception would be low-nitrogen, water-soluble fertilizers added to fungicide-insecticide sprays until early fall. Roses encouraged to grow by abundant late season fertilizing are apt to make sappy stems, which perish easily during the winter.

Organic or Chemical?

What is the difference between organic and chemical fertilizers? In the final result all organic products must undergo a chemical breakdown into basic nutrients before they are absorbed. Nitrogen from blood meal takes longer to reach growing cells than nitrogen supplied in a chemical water-soluble form. However organic fertilizers, such as fish emulsion and seaweed, contain trace elements and some soil building values.

You will improve soil by digging in humus, well-rotted manure, seaweed, grass clippings, dry organic rose fertilizers, and similar organic products. I supplement organic fertilizers with slow-release chemicals and a weak dilution of fertilizer added to any spray used on the roses. Indoors the most practical organic product is fish emulsion, but since it has a high ratio of nitrogen, use only for active plants in bright light. Too much nitrogen encourages overly rank weak growth.

Fertilizer in Warm Regions

Where winters are mild, as in southern California, Florida, or in tropical regions such as Hawaii, fertilize roses after each pruning. Bushes pruned in winter are fertilized to encourage new stems. In 6 to 8 weeks flowers will open and continue for at least a month. If you use slow-release fertilizer, it only needs to be applied every 3 to 4 months (depending on rainfall or watering).

Regular water-soluble or dry fertilizers will have to be applied after each flush of bloom for maximum flower production. In areas of low rainfall it is important to soak the soil thoroughly every few months to leach away accumulated salts from fertilizers and hard water.

Where soil is alkaline and rainfall limited, it is wise to avoid repeated applications of dried cow or steer manure. The dried manure contains high levels of chemical salts that can accumulate to cause root burn. Manure presents no problem in regions with abundant rain, since the water washes away excess salts. Carefully balanced chemical fertilizers applied in solution or as slow-release products are safe when used as directed.

Where rainfall is limited, improve soil structure with rough peat moss and compost rather than dry manure. Organically based fertilizers, with useful trace elements but no dangerous excess salts, include Espoma Rose Tone and Hoffman Rose Food (6-10-8).

MULCH

A mulch is any kind of material spread over the soil surface to protect the earth below from extremes in temperature, moisture variation, or erosion. I think a mulch also improves the general appearance of a garden. For miniature roses, which have flowers close to the ground, it is important to stop soil from splattering up during heavy rains.

By preventing soil from splashing a mulch helps keep foliage clean, and this will reduce problems from soil-borne fungus spores. Miniature rose blooms destined for the show table must be perfect, so a mulch around your favorite bushes is really a necessity. Soil covered with organic mulch is 5 to 10 degrees cooler than exposed ground.

Some gardeners apply a mulch after the roses finish their first spring bloom, thus utilizing solar heat early in the year but keeping soil cooler and holding moisture with mulch during the hot summer months.

Mulch materials suitable for roses include gravel, big chunks of redwood bark, small chips of pine bark, and salt hay.

Organic Mulches

Organic materials commonly used as mulches include bark chips and chunks, rough peat moss nuggets, shredded dry sugarcane (bagasse), buckwheat hulls, sawdust, cocoa bean hulls, ground corncobs, peanut hulls, pine needles, leaves, and compost. The compost may contain some of the other commonly used mulch materials but in a partially rotted state.

Gradual decay of these organic materials turns them into valuable humus. Once an organic mulch has rotted—which can take anywhere from six months, in warm wet climates, to two years, in colder areas—you can dig it into the soil or apply fresh mulch on top. The water holding capacity of your soil will improve, and the organic materials will provide nutrients, too.

Certain organic mulches may temporarily make some nitrogen unavailable to your roses. The bacteria, which multiply fast as they work to decompose the moist mulch, temporarily utilize some of the available nitrogen and thus cause a shortage for the roses. This is easily remedied by supplying a high-nitrogen fertilizer during the growing season.

Usually a heavy sprinkling of dried blood meal will supply an adequate nitrogen supplement, but water-soluble fertilizers are also useful. Check the section on fertilizers for details. Those mulches most likely to require an extra dose of nitrogen are sawdust and any other form of wood, such as chips, shavings, or bark. If you buy bark mulch, check the bag label, since some companies add nitrogen to make up for the bacterial action, thus saving you the trouble of adding more.

HOW TO USE MULCH

Apply mulch after bushes are planted and watered in. Spread a layer of mulch 1 to 2 inches deep around all of the shrubs, up to within an inch of the stem. Because mini roses are on their own roots (except for the tree roses), I Prefer to leave some slight space at the base until several vigorous shoots appear from below ground.

Once a mini rose is established, with 3 or more sturdy canes arising directly from the ground, push the mulch against the stems. This will help in stopping weeds. Grass and oxalis, for example, can be difficult to remove once established intertwined with the rose stems.

The depth of mulch depends on several factors: if you live in a hot dry area, mulch should be 2 inches deep and even deeper outside the branch reach of each bush (between plants). In cooler, moister regions a 1-inch layer will do. The mulch you select will also influence how deep the layer must be for full benefits.

For large chunks of material, such as bark chips or coarse pine needles, a 2-inch layer is needed; but fine, close-packing cocoa bean hulls, salt hay, or sugarcane bagasse do an adequate job with a 1-inch layer. For commercially packaged mulches check package directions for suggestions.

HOW TO CHOOSE AN ORGANIC MULCH

The mulch you select should be picked on the basis of which material you like to look at and what is locally available. In the northern states bark chips and salt hay are often the best buys, while down south sugar cane or pine needles may be best.

Now that several firms are marketing garden mulches in big plastic bags for national distribution, you can usually find at least two or three standard mulches in any region. Most popular are dark brown bark chips—usually from pine, fir, or redwood—cacao bean hulls, and buckwheat hulls. Some of the best mulch materials and their characteristics are:

BARK CHIPS: Use 1 to 2 inches deep. Chips may require additional nitrogen when bark begins to break down. Dark brown bark looks attractive, stays in place, lasts at least two years, and eventually contributes humus to the soil.

BUCKWHEAT HULLS: Apply 1 inch deep. These look light but stay put except in very strong wind. Buckwheat hulls are finer than most bark chips or cocoa mulch.

COARSE COMPOST: Compost made from wood chips, grass, leaves, fruit rinds, and a sprinkling of dried manure or well-rotted animal droppings will form a useful, enriching mulch if used in a partially rotted stage 2 to 3 inches deep. If the compost is thoroughly rotted into humus, it will evaporate almost as much moisture as bare soil and thus is not an effective mulch. However, rotted compost is useful in cold regions for hilling around bushes to protect the stems from wind and roots from heaving.

COCOA BEAN HULLS (cacao): These smell like chocolate for a few weeks but do form an effective mulch when spread 1 inch deep. They may blow in strong wind but eventually rot to form humus.

GROUND CORNCOBS: Corncobs are available in many midwestern regions. They make an excellent rose mulch when applied 1 inch deep, but the impression is not as finished or formal as is seen with salt hay or buckwheat hulls.

HAY: My favorite hay around miniatures is salt hay, widely available in coastal states but somewhat more expensive and scarce inland. The salt hay has no weed seeds and is a finely textured, uniform packing type of hay. Apply salt hay 1 to 2 inches deep. Field hay such as alfalfa and similar grasses, sold dry as stock feed, is useful but contains weed seeds or plant parts you will not want, such as bulblets of wild allium. Hay that contains manure, such as stable cleanings, is useful once it has been composted a year, but it is more properly a fertilizer.

LEAVES: Shredded leaves from hardwood trees are useful applied 1 to 2 inches deep. Dry leaves from oak trees are a fine winter mulch spread 3 to 4 inches deep. For a year-round mulch, dry leaves are rather difficult to keep in place unless sprinkled with a light layer of soil. Leaves contribute valuable humus to the soil. Oak leaves are an aid in regions where the natural soil is too alkaline, since roses do best with slightly acid soil.

Newly planted bush of 'Bonny' begins to bloom with roots and soil protected by a salt hay mulch.

PEANUT HULLS: One to 2 inches of peanut hulls form a practical mulch and eventually add a slight amount of nitrogen to the soil. They are low priced in peanut farming regions.

PEAT MOSS: The rough chunk sort of peat moss applied 1 inch deep is suitable as a mulch. Avoid fine peat moss, or even plain coarse peat moss, because this will form a nearly waterproof mat after drying out once or twice. Peat moss aids in conserving moisture and as such is useful not only as a mulch but also dug into the soil, especially in sandy soils.

PINE NEEDLES: Delightfully fragrant, pine needles spread 2 to 3 inches deep stay in place to form an attractive medium brown mulch. Roses at the American Rose Society headquarters in Louisiana are mulched with needles from the native pine trees.

SAWDUST: Around lumber mills sawdust is often available free. Applied as a 1 to 2-inch layer, it is a good mulch but temporarily robs nitrogen from the bushes. Apply supplementary nitrogen when sawdust is used.

STRAW: A 1 to 2-inch layer of coarse straw is an appealing mulch with less of a weed seed problem than hay. Oat straw is widely available and has a golden color that furnishes an unusual background for miniature roses. Eventually straw rots, to furnish useful humus. Straw bedding from rabbit hutches is a suitable mulch, but since it contains high-nitrogen manure, it should be composted at least 6 months before being used near mini roses.

SUGARCANE BAGASSE: This material is often sold as poultry litter, since it absorbs moisture so well. Bagasse is crushed and ground sugarcane, a by-product of sugar refining, more available in our southern states than elsewhere. I like the light brown color and slightly smokey smell of bagasse. Applied as a 1-inch deep layer, it is an effective, durable mulch.

Inorganic Mulch

An inorganic mulch often lasts longer than organic soil coverings. Plastic, for example, may eventually tear, but the actual material will endure several years, particularly if lightly covered with soil to stop it from blowing about or ripping.

Gravel lasts almost forever, but cultivation and replanting will eventually mix it with the top soil. Paving stones, slate, cement blocks, cinders—all can be employed to cover exposed soil, stop spattering of flowers, and hold soil moisture.

HOW TO CHOOSE AN INORGANIC MULCH

Which inorganic mulch you prefer will depend on your general garden design. Informal gardens do not lend themselves to carefully placed plastic mulch, but black or clear plastic film disguised with pine bark or salt hay might fit in.

White gravel fits well into a formal setting. The light color helps keep soil cool and is therefore an advantage in hot climates. Bluestone, granite chips, and washed pebbles in mixed cream to yellow tones are less conspicuous than the white marble chips. In areas where soil is very alkaline it would be best to avoid using marble, because these chips have a slow sweeting action. In very acid soils, on the other hand, this reaction may be a useful one.

Commercial growers use plastic film as a soil mulch to prevent weeds, capture solar heat to warm roots, and drastically slow down water evaporation from the soil. Soil temperatures are 5 to 10 degrees warmer under plastic than if the soil is left bare.

Here miniature roses are mulched with gravel, stones, and a thin layer of humus.

Since the plastic film also stops rain from getting through, it is important to have an open area around the stem so that rain can reach roots. A soaker hose under the plastic mulch will further insure adequate moisture. Black plastic is good as a weed stopper, but clear plastic actually encourages weeds by acting like a greenhouse.

Plastic mulch is efficient, but I find it unattractive in a garden setting. If it is the most reasonably priced mulch for your area (dry regions and where organic materials may be too expensive), you can still enjoy the advantages of plastic without distracting from a natural garden picture. Just cover the plastic with a thin layer of organic mulch, such as hay or straw.

In windy regions gravel or soil must cover the plastic to prevent constant displacement. Consider the advantages and disadvantages of each mulch material easily obtained in your town, then choose a product best suited to the garden design and your personal taste.

Around my waterside garden in southern New York I use several different mulches to fit in with various plantings. A raised bed built on deeply grooved glacial rock has large 2 to 3-inch chunks of pine bark around a rainbow of mini roses. In another area I created a more intricate Oriental-style terraced setting, where fine spruce needles and some thin bark chips seem more in place. Mini roses planted near shrubs or among perennials are mulched with salt hay.

A few mini roses against the greenhouse wall are mulched with a twenty-year accumulation of half-rotted orchid compost, the product of repotting hundreds of plants growing in fir bark, perlite, tree fern, and hardwood charcoal. Soil in these beds has been improved with leaf mold, coarse peat moss, vermiculite, and perlite.

Renewal

Organic mulches should be renewed whenever weeds begin to grow through or the protective layer fails to hide bare earth. Inorganic materials need renewal on the same basis, but less often.

In temperate climates with hard winters, soil heaving and heavy rains may make twice yearly (spring and fall) renewals necessary. Organic mulches gradually improve soil structure, so nothing is lost, although renewal of the surface is required. A mulch complements good soil preparation, but no mulch will compensate for poor soil.

7
Garden Display and Design

You will enjoy miniature roses for their long blooming season: May to October in cold regions, or April into December where winters are mild. With such a constant display it is no wonder that many growers create special sections in the garden just for miniature roses.

A planting devoted to mini roses will simplify routine care. If you grow roses for show, the formal planting will help you keep track of names. Even with labels near garden plants, I make maps of each section, recording plant locations. No matter how carefully I label plants, some tags always disappear or fade just when I want to double-check a variety name. Keeping your roses carefully recorded and organized in their own sunny, well-drained beds will be a big help when show time comes or a friend asks, "What rose is that?"

Certainly some of the ultra-tiny hybrids like 'Si' or 'Littlest Angel' will be lost if planted among assorted garden perennials. Only in carefully tended raised beds or rock gardens of dwarf species do micro minis have much chance to survive. Larger modern mini hybrids are more vigorous but still deserve protection from encroaching neighbors. My drawing of an underground root barrier (chapter 5) shows how to save mini roses from damaging root competition.

DESIGN

The actual design of a rose planting can reflect your personal taste. Once you provide the cultural basics of good soil, adequate drainage, and bright light, you should arrange the bushes to suit yourself. Some interesting mini rose gardens are shown in my photos.

Miniature roses provide a welcome touch of color in a sunny lawn border.

Clean, clear lines, carefully placed labels, redwood steps, and bark mulch make this Texas miniature rose display a true showpiece.

Raised pyramid beds protect small roses and simplify care. A bark mulch and precise labeling complete this West Virginia planting.

In this Kansas garden, miniature roses are featured in an original terrace. Climbing miniatures decorate open trellises and stone steps provide easy access. (Photo by Larry Heilman)

Miniature roses can create an easy-to-care-for border along a garden path. Hanging baskets of roses, soon to begin blooming, decorate the bird feeder pole in the background.

A miniature rose garden, designed by Margaret Pinney in Renaissance style, ready for a winter rest.

The same garden starting growth in the spring with several roses already in bloom.

One charming idea carried out by mini rose grower Margaret Pinney is a formal rectangular garden in Renaissance style. Upright dwarf evergreen junipers grow at each end of a narrow bed. In the center is a pool featuring small water lilies during the growing season. In scale with tiny roses are miniature reproductions of classic statues, situated in a semicircular nook around the garden boundry.

When seen as an isolated garden, without visual reference to larger plants, it is difficult to realize that this whole formal bed is less than 3 by 5 feet. The secret of this perfect balance is in selecting accessories and companion plants in scale with the 3 to 8-inch tall rosebushes.

INTEGRATED PLANTINGS

Certain modern hybrids regularly grow 18 to 24 inches tall and almost as wide when given rich soil and moderate pruning. A plant of 'Baby Mas-

Miniature roses are well integrated with a relaxed garden plan at the home of mini rose hobbyist Frances M. Mannell. (Photo by Larry Heilman)

A weathered cypress fence forms a pleasant background for this restrained design by Dave Lajoie featuring miniature roses, dwarf yews, and a *Sedum glaucum* ground cover. The raised bed provides sharp drainage and easy working height.

querade' just outside of my greenhouse is 35 inches tall and 22 inches wide, even with root competition.

Meilland's 'White Gem', Moore's 'Fire Princess' and 'Magic Carrousel', and Dot's 'Baby Gold Star' are some other vigorous hybrids that can make a show in mixed plantings. For example, a bush of brilliant red 'Fire Princess' given good soil and direct sun will create quite a show near dwarf yellow marigolds or when viewed against the silver leaves of creeping snow-in-summer (*Cerastium tomentosum*).

I have an 18-inch bush of 'White Gem' planted so that flowers are seen with a dark green mugho pine in the background. Pink-flowered 'Judy Fischer' and 'Mimi' are lovely near dwarf blue platycodon. When you plant roses near other perennials, or even large annuals, you must provide extra fertilizer and water. Without additional food and moisture the small roses will sit still or perhaps even die.

LIMITED BARRIERS

Some protection can be given individual roses in mixed plantings by pushing slate slabs or thin rocks into the soil around each mini bush. When preparing the hole, set the mini barriers to provide an 8 to 10-inch space

Just-planted mini rose bed has small terraces and spruce needle mulch. Underground barriers keep out roots from companion plants.

Raised metal edging provides protection for a collection of miniature roses sharing garden space with vegetables and larger roses.

around small minis, 12 to 15 inches for vigorous hybrids. Push the barriers at least 8 inches deep. Make barriers flush with the soil level unless you want to see the defined area. A projection about 1 inch above soil level is easily hidden later by mulch.

RAISED BEDS

Making a raised bed is another way to keep competing roots away from your roses, even when other garden plants are right nearby. Natural stone walls, constructed with a firm foundation and good drainage, are an excellent way to form a 1 to 3-foot deep raised bed anywhere.

On slopes a raised bed may be built with only three sides. Raised beds are easy to care for since plants are at a higher level. For maximum convenience build the bed at waist level, thus forming a garden where you will not have to kneel, and where the flowers will be closer and therefore the fragrance more powerful. Raised beds are perfect along sunken garden paths, sloping driveways, or between lawn and beach at the shore.

On a slope in any sunny area mini roses can provide constant color. This recently planted collection greets visitors to the home of miniature rose specialist John Ewing.

A raised bed on bedrock where I used three different levels to fully utilize space. Although built on rock, the bed has excellent drainage through glacial scrapes leading to the cove in the background.

A boulder is used as focal point for roses, backed by yellow evening primroses and iris.

This West Virginia backyard has been transformed into a showplace of miniature roses. Trailing types grow in baskets, others in lawn beds edged with metal or in borders.

Where you will view a planting from only one or two sides, stage hybrids according to height. By placing taller growers toward the back, even tiny treasures like 'Si' can always be seen. However, for an artistic arrangement with some surprises, you may want to hide part of the planting from a certain angle.

A tall rose toward the front or perhaps a craggy rock or driftwood piece can effectively create depth. As you change position by arcing around, new vistas will open up, thus forming a more intriguing design than two-dimensional staging.

Rocks, sculpture, fountains, and driftwood will not compete with roots, but they can cause undesirable shade if placed poorly. Choose moderately sized objects and situate them so that the roses receive all the sun possible. Only in hot dry regions might shade over roses be desirable—at midday in Arizona or southern Florida, for example.

TIERS

Some miniature rose gardeners stuff hundreds of plants into a few square feet by building beds several tiers high. These tiered gardens are sometimes offered in catalogs as rolls of corrugated metal, 5 to 8 inches

Sturdy metal forms a raised pyramid garden, where the roses will soon hide all construction details. Creeping sedum also trails over the metal later in the season. (Photo by Larry Heilman)

tall, often sold as strawberry towers. The same arrangement will serve as a pyramid for mini rosebushes. Bricks, redwood, cement blocks, or railroad ties form long-lasting tiered beds but are harder to work with and more expensive than the rather short-lived metal rolls.

To begin, start out with a circle, square, or rectangle about 4 feet across. The material you use will determine how long your raised bed lasts. Metal lawn edging and flexible corrugated aluminum rolls sold for making raised pyramid beds will shift and bend, especially in climates where soil freezes in winter. Stones, slate, or cement blocks, held by a cement backing, will last many years.

CONSTRUCTION

Begin construction of a raised-tier bed by assuring sharp drainage on the foundation level. Dig down about 8 to 10 inches and set in several inches of coarse gravel, such as 1 to 2-inch size bluestone, lava rock, or whatever stone is most reasonably priced in your neighborhood. Cover this drainage layer with a mixture of 50 percent leaf mold or humus and 50 percent coarse sphagnum peat moss.

Fill the circle with topsoil prepared as outlined in chapter 5. Water and allow to settle for a day. Tamp soil until firm, then set tier number two in the center, with the base 3 to 4 inches deep. Add 2 inches of humus–peat moss mix, fill with soil, and repeat for each tier.

Miniature roses look lovely as featured plants set in lawn beds, here defined with cement patio blocks.

One nice way to provide privacy is to cover a fence with climbing miniature roses, possible even in small gardens. These newly planted miniatures will soon cover the fence with a shower of fragrant flowers.

Climbing miniatures provide height and conserve space by growing on background supports, while carefully labeled bush hybrids fill the foreground section, in the garden of John Ewing, Chairman of the A.R.S. Miniature Rose Testing Program.

For practical reasons the top tier should be at least 2 feet across. Each tier can be 8 to 12 inches tall. A good average height is 10 inches, since this provides enough root run for minis without causing undue shade or creating a disturbing grossness of scale.

If you wish to simplify watering, install a water pipe under the bottom layer and up through the center. The pipe can be metal or plastic. At the top use a standard hose male end to which you can attach the nozzle or hose desired. For example with a 2-foot length of hose at the top you could add a brass rectangular sprinkler or similar sprinkler.

If watering overhead causes black-spot problems in your area, install a six-tube Soakeze device to water at ground level, or spread a canvas soaking hose under the plants to assure even watering at all tier levels.

Underground watering tubes with bubbler nozzles, spaced every 12 to 15 inches, will permit easy watering with no foliage wetting at all. If you are constructing a mini rose bed from scratch, consider installing some of this underground pipe. The system is similar to underground lawn sprinkling devices except that the water nozzles are designed to bubble out rather than create a wide-spreading spray.

'Baby Masquerade' as a 26-inch tall shrub

'Seabreeze' is a recent hybrid with enough vigor to form a border hedge. Stems easily reach 25 to 28 inches, and have clusters of pink flowers.

BORDERS AND HEDGES

Bushy hybrids such as 'Baby Masquerade', 'Cinderella', and 'Anytime' are suitable as low hedges or formal borders. In rich, deeply dug soil the vigorous miniatures can be expected to grow at least 18 inches in a season, often 24 to 30 inches if kept well watered and fertilized. Most gardeners do not want their miniatures to grow so fast or so tall, but for a hedge this is a useful option.

Since even the minis have thorns and reasonably stiff branches, they form, after two seasons, a barrier not easily passed. Where sunlight is adequate, it is much nicer to have a fragrant flowering rose border or mini hedge than to waste sunny growing space on plain foliage plants.

For a thick line, plant mini roses 8 inches apart. After a summer of growth it will be hard to tell one plant from another. If you have no need for a dense "stay out" type of hedge, then space plants 12 to 15 inches apart. With the wider spacing each bush can branch out naturally, and the appearance is more graceful. In small gardens or narrow boundary lines, the larger miniature rose hybrids are less of a problem to maintain than floribunda roses or hybrid teas.

OUTDOOR CONTAINERS

Miniatures are unusual subjects in window boxes, garden urns, decorative terrace pots, redwood boxes, and patio planters. In milder climates, where winters do not have deep freezes, miniatures are often featured in containers. Where winters are severe, containers must be large enough to prevent complete freezing. The freezing and occasional midwinter thawing can harm even the toughest miniatures.

During the spring, summer, and fall you can enjoy miniatures in outdoor containers anywhere you garden. I have some favorite clones in big window boxes on the terrace, where the bushes offer fragrant flowers all season long. In the winter I mulch these bushes with a thick layer of salt hay. Bushes in smaller window boxes, such as those fashioned from wooden wine crates, must be planted in garden beds or kept in a frost-free location to be completely safe from cold winters.

A Texas patio decorated with miniature roses, some in a strawberry jar; climbing roses are on the background fence.

WINDOW BOXES

Miniature climbers are nice in window boxes, where there is room for the long stems to trail. Any of the hybrids listed as climbers (see chapter 4) are suitable. Long window boxes used as terrace planters look lovely with climbers trailing over each end, while bushy upright miniatures fill in the center sections. For small window boxes you might feature micro minis (see chapter 3). With all window box containers be sure that drainage remains sharp.

I put a layer of gravel and some chunks of hardwood charcoal in the bottom of each window box, then cover this with unmilled sphagnum moss, a useful method for all outdoor containers. To avoid troubles with pests

Left: This wooden wine crate will make an attractive, long-lasting window box. First treat with Cuprinol to preserve wood. Strips of wood are nailed across the bottom for air circulation and drainage freedom. *Right:* Use a plastic garbage bag to line the crate. Make holes in the bottom of the plastic for drainage.

Left: Add an inch of gravel to keep drainage free. *Right:* Fill the new window box with professionally prepared planting mix as outlined in chapter 12.

Below: Water planting mix with warm water. Allow newly filled window box to settle a day before planting. *Right:* This window box, created by Murrie Marden Fitch, was partially painted with redwood stain, but the vineyard name was left for decoration. Note how important bottom strips keep the window box slightly raised.

often found in garden soil, fill the window boxes with a clean commercial potting mix. Terra-Lite Rose Bush Planting Soil is one suitable brand, professionally formulated with vermiculite, sphagnum peat moss, and a slow-release fertilizer.

Other suitable container fillings include versions of peat-lite mix such as Pro-Mix, Jiffy-Mix, and similar soil-free formulas. These handy mixes are highly satisfactory when combined with a slow-release fertilizer.

PLANT PORTABILITY

A popular system with some growers is to cultivate miniature roses in 6 to 8-inch pots but bury the pots under peat moss in a long redwood planter or similar trough. This permits quick shifting of any plant, without the trouble of digging up roots. Any individual bush that you wish to shift, turn, or replace need only be lifted out with its own pot. The vacancy can be quickly filled with another potted specimen. This is also an easy way to summer mini roses that you wish to keep in pots for growing inside later.

With this pot-in-a-trough system it is important that both the individual pot and the trough or window box have adequate drainage. If you garden in an area with limited rainfall or wish to reduce the frequency of watering outdoor containers, use some hydrogel in the potting mix, as is explained in chapter 4 for baskets.

ROOT PRUNING

If you wish to maintain bushes in 6 to 8-inch pots more than a season, it is helpful to prune some of the roots at the same time you prune back the branches. For example, in California, where miniatures are frequently kept in pots the year around, growers will prune back the tops, cut back about one-third of the roots, then repot into fresh mix—all in the cooler season, around January or February.

This is similar to the technique used on bonsai trees, but not as extreme. Roots are also pruned back on bushes that you dig up for growing indoors during the winter, to balance the plant after top pruning.

Crocus 'Peter Pan', a pure white early-spring companion to my miniature roses

8
Companions in
the Garden

With the first crocus of spring and on through the late fall mums and the Christmas-roses (hellebores), your miniature roses can be joined by restrained companions that flower when true roses are not in bloom. By selecting companion plants with care your mini rose bed will always have something of beauty on display.

The most vigorous miniatures can usually fend for themselves in mixed plantings, along the front of perennial borders, or even among smaller perennials. However, the more restrained miniatures such as the micro minis are best accompanied by equally restrained companions from other flower families.

SPRING

Your garden will herald spring a month before the official date, even where winters are cold, if you plant early-flowering bulbs. While miniature roses are still dormant, the first snowdrops, crocus, and sunny yellow Eranthis will begin opening—sometimes even through the snow. For an extra-early show, plant these bulbs at the base of walls, where the solar heat absorbed by the stones will help them along.

It is easier to obtain a succession of color in the garden by selecting plants that grow during different parts of the season. Bulbs are thus definitely useful with miniature roses.

The first to appear are usually crocus. Nearly every year *Crocus imperati* pushes through the snow on bright January and February days, sometimes getting knocked down by a late winter snowstorm. Tiny bulbs, such as the crocus species and miniature daffodils, can safely be planted within inches

Hosta tardiflora grows slowly into a tight clump of dark green glossy leaves, forming a plant 6 to 8 inches tall. Lavender blue flowers appear in midfall.

of miniature roses. By the time roses need the space for new growth, the bulb foliage is ready to die back. After a few years the bulbs will come up through the outer branches of established roses, but neither plant will suffer.

Crocus species are excellent to tuck among mini roses, along edges of beds, or in window box displays. As with other small bulbs, you will find the widest selection listed in specialized catalogs such as de Jager (see lists in chapter 19). Also check with your local garden store in September and October, when bulbs are on display. The autumn-flowering crocus species are an exception in that you will find these offered for sale in late summer.

Crocus speciosus 'Oxonian' is a garden surprise; it blooms in September.

Snowdrops *(Galanthus nivalis)*

White, yellow, lavender, purple, and combinations of lilac, yellow, and dark brown, as in *C. imperati,* are the available colors in crocus species. The hybrids have much larger flowers but are suitable with mini roses if kept 8 to 10 inches away. For the most colorful display, to border a rose bed for example, the larger hybrid crocus are outstanding. Fine choices include the huge pure white 'Peter Pan', showy purple and white striped 'Pickwick', and silvery blue 'Little Dorrit'.

Snowdrops *(Galanthus* species) will bloom along with early crocus. The popular single snowdrop *(G. nivalis)* is about 6 inches tall; the larger-flowered *G. elwesii* reaches 10 inches, has 1-inch white and green nodding bell-shaped flowers, and thrives in sun but tolerates shade.

Bulbous iris take little space and die back before roses reach their prime. For late February and early March flowers, plant *Iris reticulata* and its hybrids; all have fragrant flowers in shades of dark purple to light blue, on 6-inch tall plants. The 3-inch tall *I. danfordiae,* with yellow flowers, is a nice contrast in front of the taller purple or blue *I. reticulata* selections.

Yellow winter aconite (*Eranthis hyemalis*) opens in late February. The flowers resemble big buttercups but appear on low 2 to 3-inch tall light green plants against a corona of green leaflets. Aconite seeds form readily, so small colonies may develop. Plant the tubers 2 inches deep, setting them at the base of a south-facing rock for earliest flowering.

Chionodoxa bloom almost as early as aconites, usually by the first week in March, just after the first crocus and bulbous iris. Chionodoxa quickly form clumps of bulbs and even reseed around, but plants are a restrained 3 to 4 inches tall, no real competition for miniature roses. The flowers are

Chinodoxa gigantea

Narcissus minimus

Scilla tubergeniana, a light blue miniature flower for early spring; plant bulbs in the fall.

Milla biflora grows from bulbs, produces slate-blue flowers in early spring, has flat, strap-shaped leaves that taste of garlic; also sold as *Triteleia* and *Ipheion.*

starry, pale violet with a lighter center in *Chionodoxa gigantea*, to deep blue with a white center in *C. luciliae*. I have one form called *C.* 'Pink Giant' that has pale pink flowers. The smallest and most intense blue is in *C. sardensis*.

Near the blue chionodoxa, miniature daffodils are a fine contrast in shape and color. First in my garden is the 3-inch tall *Narcissus minimus* (*N. asturiensis*) with butter yellow ½-inch flowers. *N. cyclamineus* has sharply reflexed petals usually opening by mid-March, and slightly taller 6-inch stems.

From time to time bulb specialists offer other charming miniature daffodil species such as *N. bulbocodium* (6 to 8 inches tall) and *N. juncifolius* (4 to 5 inches tall). Order these if you can find them, as they are well worth growing along the edges of your mini rose beds or tucked into spaces between big rocks in terraced rose plantings. Combine miniature daffodil flowers from the garden with flowers of roses grown indoors for striking spring arrangements. Most miniature roses will be bigger than tiny *N. minimus.*

MIDSPRING INTO SUMMER

As April fades into May, the bulbs begin to give way to other perennials, such as the dainty columbines (*Aquilegia*). Dwarf columbines come in white, blue, and pink. I love the 6-inch tall *A. flabellata,* a species from Japan with blue or white flowers. This restrained grower will seed about but never becomes a pest. *A. alpina* has dark purple blue flowers about the time miniature roses begin to bloom. Try this next to yellow roses.

The tall 15 to 24-inch spires of coralbells (*Heuchera*) look lovely behind mini rose plants. Since the heucheras grow well in shade, you can place them toward the back of mini rose beds even if light is dimmer there. The heucheras form 2 to 4-inch pads of round green leaves, but the flower spikes are tall and airy, opening into white, pink, or coral-toned flowers.

Geranium sanguineum prostratum

The newer strains of *Iberis* produce 4 to 6-inch tall mounds of stark white flowers in May to early June and compact foliage the rest of the year. 'Purity' and 'Little Gem' are two good dwarf types of *Iberis*.

Another fine plant for terraces of rock gardens is the dwarf carnation or pink. I grow these from seed sown along the rock walls, but quicker, more precise effects are had by planting clumps from flats or pots in early spring. Species *Dianthus alpinus* and *D. deltoides* are low carpets with dainty white to dark pink flowers. The various hybrid Cheddar pinks (*D. gratianopolitanus*) in shades of pink are also suitable along the edges of rose beds.

Geranium sanguineum prostratum (*G. lancastriense*) reminds me of a dianthus, since it has single, flat pink flowers and a creeping growth 2 to 3 inches tall. Flowers appear from May into September. This is a truly cold-hardy geranium that thrives in a sunny, well-drained location. The multilobed leaves are deep green all summer and turn orange to red with cool fall weather.

SUCCULENTS

Several succulent plants are useful in rock garden or stone wall mini rose beds. Sedums provide ground cover and flowers in the same space. *Sedum glaucum* is a restrained pale gray mat. Blue green *S. dasyphyllum* is another 2-inch tall creeper that is safe around miniature plantings. Taller sedums are suitable toward the back of rose beds.

Sempervivums grow as symmetrical rosettes, with 2 to 6-inch spikes of starry pink or white flowers, clusters of plantlets around the main crown, thus fostering the popular name of Hen and Chicks.

A restrained type is *S. arachnoideum*, which looks as though its center were woven of fine cobwebs. Among the many hybrids of sempervivum are some that grow to 8 inches across. Several have metallic purple foliage. All are worthwhile in rock gardens or any well-drained sunny location with rather restricted root run. These are trouble-free gems that will complement your mini rose garden without ever becoming invasive.

A succulent annual that often reseeds is *Portulaca grandiflora*. New dwarf hybrid strains bloom quickly from seed, grow 4 to 6 inches tall, and bloom all summer long. The flowers actually resemble miniature roses, especially the double portulacas. The plants come in many colors including rose, yellow, white, and combinations. Sow seed where these are to grow, or obtain started plants in flats from your local garden stores in the spring.

Sempervivums form a living waterfall among pumice stones.

Sempervivum arachnoideum thrives in a sunny rock crack with limited soil in a wall of my raised mini rose bed.

Orostachys spinosa is a low silvery green succulent to grow in rock cracks or similar places with sharp drainage and full sun. It is fully cold hardy in my New York garden.

LILIES

Dwarf lilies are useful for color, fragrance, and some height near mini roses. Lilies thrive with their roots shaded and their tops in the sun. The upright growth seldom interferes with mini roses, but in windy locations stems may have to be staked.

The species *Lilium concolor* has waxy red orange flowers on sturdy 12 to 15-inch stems and grows easily from seed, flowering the second year. Lilies thrive with the same well-drained, slightly acid soil favored by roses. Extra peat moss and leaf mold are suitable soil supplements around lilies. Mulch as recommended for roses.

Some new hybrid selections from world famous Oregon Bulb Farms (formerly the Jan de Graaff lily farm) are appropriately dwarf. These new selections have been bred for adaptability and floriferousness. A useful way to place them is toward the back of your roses. In the case of terraced plantings or displays in front of stone walls, the lilies will appreciate bottom shade from the roses. Excellent choices include:

'CONNECTICUT LEMONGLOW', a July-blooming hybrid, has clear gold flowers on 20 to 24-inch stems.

'HARLEQUIN' hybrids, an early to mid-July-flowering strain that grows three to four feet tall, is well suited for planting behind mini rose beds. 'Harlequin' lilies come in mixed colors ranging from yellow to deep orange, all with recurved form and black dots.

'LITTLE RASCAL' strain lilies bloom from late July into August on stout 18 to 22-inch stems. The 4 to 5-inch flowers are like miniature auratum lilies, with the same intoxicating perfume. This sturdy, deliciously scented strain has basically white flowers marked with gold, pink, or red rays and a sprinkling of orange dots. Truly one of the most pleasing and practical new lilies in years.

'PASTEL' strain hybrids grow only 12 to 18 inches tall but produce an abundance of wide, outward-facing 3 to 4-inch flowers in delicate shades of pink, cream, or yellow with coffee-brown spots.

'SUNKISSED' is an outstanding clone for vigor and an abundance of medium orange flowers on sturdy 30 to 36-inch stems that bloom in mid to late June.

The lilies mentioned above will thrive in large pots, which makes precise garden placement possible. Pot the bulbs in 6 to 8-inch heavy plastic or rubber nursery containers in the spring. When plants develop, you can

A light apricot 'Pastel' strain lily towers above one of my mini rose beds but does not conflict with rose growth.

'Harlequin' strain lily with butter yellow flowers

'Little Rascal' strain lily with red markings

'Sunkissed' lily

place the lilies in a garden location that best suits the lily height, color, and season.

Some local garden centers also offer container-grown lilies for planting anytime during the growing season. When planting, just remove the whole soil ball by turning the pot upside down and drop the complete ball with roots into a hole of the same depth without disturbing the lily roots.

ANNUALS

Dwarf annuals are suitable for filling in bare spaces near miniature roses and in front of raised beds. It is an easy matter to hide metal or cinder-block bed foundations by planting bushy, colorful annuals in the spring.

Local garden centers offer annuals, often already in bloom. These professionally grown plants are a good buy. With reasonable care they will provide color all season long. Some suitable compact annuals include:

AGERATUM (*Ageratum mexicanum*) hybrids in blue ('Blue Angel') or white ('Summer Snow') grow 6 to 8 inches.

ALYSSUM (*Lobularia maritima*) hybrids, such as 'Tiny Tim', which matures at 3 inches and has masses of white flowers until frost.

BEGONIA (*Begonia semperflorens*) hybrids in dwarf strains grow 6 to 8 inches tall and have flowers until frost. Slightly taller, to 10 inches, but covered with large flowers, are new Glamour hybrids offered in pink, red, rose, and unusual white with pink edge called Picotee.

COLEUS in new 'Carefree' or 'Saber' hybrids grow but 6 to 10 inches tall and provide colorful fill between rows or hide construction details of raised beds.

DIANTHUS hybrids of annual strains now come in 3 to 6-inch tall types with very bushy growth. Examples are 'Wee Willie' and 'Baby Doll', both in mixed shades of pink, white, and red.

MARIGOLDS with very low growth include various strains of French marigolds in yellow, orange, and new blended colors on 6 to 8-inch plants. Check national seed catalogs prepared by major seed producers such as Burpee and Park for new introductions.

IMPATIENS are useful to fill in shady sections of the garden, although they will live in full sun. New Elfin hybrids grow into 8-inch mounds covered with flat open flowers and are available in many colors from white to pink shades and true red. My favorite is red and white 'Twinkles'.

WINTER

In cold climates the garden goes to sleep in winter, but miniature rose beds can still be interesting if you have a few evergreen heathers nearby. Because some of the heathers grow as tall as the miniature roses, you will want to keep them in different beds, slightly below the roses in terraced plantings, or, alternatively, plant only the smallest heathers. Some good compact sorts that are easy to prune by clipping with shears just before spring growth begins, include:

CALLUNA VULGARIS 'MRS. J. H. HAMILTON', a rose pink that has tiny spires of flowers summer into fall.

CALLUNA VULGARIS 'MRS. R. H. GRAY' creeps along 2 to 3 inches tall with dark green evergreen needlelike foliage and pink flowers from July into September.

Related to the heathers are the heaths, equally useful for winter color and unusual contrasts to the rosebushes.

ERICA CARNEA 'VIVELLI' seldom gets above 10 inches tall and has bronze green foliage and very intense rose flowers from midwinter to May.

lchicum 'Waterlily' has pink flowers in the fall as the garden is going to rest. nt colchicum bulbs in early fall. Leave 12 to 18 inches between mini roses and 175
lbs because early-season colchicum foliage grows to a foot tall.

Colchicum 'Lilac Wonder' blooms in late September.

ERICA CARNEA 'SPRINGWOOD WHITE' is a vigorous, spreading grower but easy to control. It generally reaches 8 to 10 inches tall and has needlelike foliage and tiny white flowers from midwinter into spring.

Heathers and heaths like sunny, well-drained acid soil. Once established, they seldom require any care except the spring "haircut" to keep them neat and some water if there are long periods without any rain. Both calluna and erica provide charming green branches to fill in arrangements of miniature rose flowers.

Roses 'Perla de Montserrat' and 'Wee Lass' with a budded branch of *Erica carnea* 'Sherwoodii' and *Calluna vulgaris* 'Else Frye', a double white pompom

'White Angel' has many stems in the fall. These should be left until spring, then pruned.

9
Seasonal Calendar
of Care

Culture of garden roses is necessarily related to the seasons. Hawaii, southern Florida, and a few very mild regions in California have no truly cold months, but even these areas have variations in temperature and rainfall according to the time of year.

For most gardeners the four seasons of our temperate region determine how we care for outdoor roses. Even within the temperate zone we have variations in actual dates for the last frost, early daffodil bloom, first fall frost, and other weather events. Watching your miniature roses through a full garden year will help tailor this calendar of seasonal care to your own micro climate.

EARLY SPRING (MARCH OR WHEN GROUND IS THAWED)

1. Prepare new planting sites.

2. Order roses you forgot to order during the winter.

3. Plant dormant roses received from mail order firms or local garden centers.

4. Water newly planted roses thoroughly—every week unless it rains.

5. Gradually wash away soil mounds if you use earth as winter protection around bushes.

6. Prune back damaged branches to live buds. Wait until buds begin to grow if you are not sure which are alive.

7. Spray all bushes with fungicide on a mild day, 50° to 60°F.

8. Add all-purpose insecticide (e.g., Isotox) to fungicide spray if pests are a serious problem in your garden.

9. Check undersides of foliage on indoor roses for signs of spider mites.

Pruning tools useful for roses include: *center,* large Wilkinson #70 shears for long-term garden use; *lower left,* the Mini Corona #6 shears (only 5 inches long); *lower right,* small cuticle scissors; *top right,* snub-nosed pocket pruner from Brookstone Co. The snub-nosed pruners are stainless steel, have one serrated jaw, and fit into a pocket without making holes.

Pruning Tools

Spring is the time to be sure you have the correct pruning tools. Precision pruning shears with sharpened blades assure clean cuts. Quick-healing clean cuts minimize problems from infection or damaged buds. My favorite precision shears are made by Wilkinson Sword Company, who though originally of England, are now offering several sizes of shears in the United States. For small, delicate work the pointed Corona thinning shears Model 21-S and 21-C Grape Shear are perfect.

Indoors even a sharp pair of long-handled stainless steel scissors are practical. However, for thick stems the scissors will not have enough leverage to make a smooth cut. A pair of mini shears, such as the 5-inch long Mini Corona No. 6, is handy for grooming indoor roses.

Pruning Techniques

Sharp, well-designed pruning tools will make clean cuts where you want them. There is no need to paint cuts on pruned miniature roses. Make each pruning cut about ¼ inch above a dormant bud. Cut at a slight slant, about 45 degrees, if you are dealing with a major branch or main stem.

For thin twigs there is no need to be compulsive about cutting at a slant. The slanted cut sheds water and sprays more quickly than straight cuts, therefore reducing the chance of rot starting when a wound remains moist. However, with healthy mini roses in sunny gardens such precision pruning is unnecessary. More important than the precise angle of cut is the technique of cutting to just above a bud so that no long, growthless stem section is left to die and decay.

Look to the general shape of each bush and thin out overly thick inner branches. The hybrid at hand will determine how drastically you prune. The micro minis hardly need any pruning. In contrast, a vigorous sort, such as 'Baby Masquerade' or 'Magic Carrousel', will have to be pruned in spring and again as you trim flowering during the season. Wearing gloves makes pruning work go faster, since you can grab stems anywhere without danger of being thorned.

MID-SPRING (APRIL OR ONCE LEAVES OPEN)

1. Plant indoor roses outside after a week of gradual outdoor exposure. Roses in full leaf will usually sunburn when transplanted directly from in-

A growing shoot of 'Orange Fire' sprouted five new shoots when the tip was pinched. Pinching produces more compact, bushy roses.

181

doors to the garden unless they are protected. I use leafy branches pruned from shrubs or trees for temporary shade. Salt hay or straw will also work as shade if your garden is not too windy.

2. Renew mulch around roses.

3. Fertilize all bushes as leaf buds swell.

4. Finish final spring pruning.

5. Prune back competing shrubs to provide full sun and air circulation around your miniatures.

6. Plant baskets, terrace tubs, and window boxes with roses.

7. Continue spray program you favor.

8. If you do not use fungicides or insecticides, then use vigorous plain water spray every few days from the hose.

LATE SPRING (ROSES WILL BE IN FULL BLOOM NOW)

1. Cut flowers as buds show color, about ¼ open, for enjoyment indoors.

2. Check garden centers for container-grown miniatures in bloom. You can plant potted roses all season long.

3. Fertilize with balanced rose food.

Snip off faded blooms just above a complete leaf. Make the cut about ¼ inch above a dormant stem bud. The bud will grow into a new flowering shoot.

Roses near warm foundations will often bloom longer into fall than bushes in the open garden. Careful grooming keeps climbers and bush hybrids neat near this home pathway.

4. Be on the lookout for mildew and black spot, likely to appear with warm, moist weather. Spray with fungicides every week as prevention (see chapter 10 for compromise).

5. Cut off faded flowers back to first complete leaf.

6. Make controlled crosses if you want to grow roses from your own garden seed. Hips need all season to ripen (see chapter 16).

SUMMER (WARMEST SEASON, OFTEN DRY)

1. Keep roses well watered (see chapter 6).

2. Prune after each flush of bloom.

3. Make cuttings from ripe branches (see chapter 16).

4. Control spider mites wih strong water spray from hose, or apply insecticides. Spider mites thrive during warm, dry weather.

5. Apply final soil fertilizers no later than mid-August in regions where winters are freezing. Late feeding encourages easily frozen new growth.

6. Check climbers for proper pruning and training. Be sure supports are sturdy. Tie long canes to supports with plastic-coated wire or heavy string.

FALL (NIGHTS DROP BELOW 50°F., GROWTH SLOWS)

1. Prepare new beds for fall planting (where winters are not severe) or to mellow until spring planting.
2. Take cuttings for propagations to grow indoors.
3. Apply any sprays you use. I apply Benlate and Phaltan with a solution of weak low-nitrogen fertilizer in the late fall but while roses still have leaves (October in New York).

LATE FALL INTO EARLY WINTER (BEFORE GROUND IS HARD)

1. Dig up bushes you want indoors. Trim roots and tops about one-third off, pot, sink containers in moist peat moss or sand outdoors. An alternative is to put dormant bushes in warmest part of refrigerator. Provide 6 to 8 weeks of cool rest, then grow roses indoors (see chapters 11 and 12).
2. Secure climber canes to prevent injury from wind and snow.
3. Mulch bare soil around bushes.
4. In regions with severe winters protect plant base with soil or hay.

Winter Protection

Over most of the temperate zone temperatures drop below freezing and stay there for several months. During this season miniature roses are susceptible to mechanical injury from ice, heavy snow, and gnawing creatures such as mice or rabbits. The injury from small animals can be prevented by enclosing roses behind fences or protecting them with various types of cover.

Some growers use bottles with the ends cut out, others prefer rose cones, baskets, upturned crates. I prefer to use nothing. Slight injury from mice or ice correspond to pruning. If a bush is healthy below ground, it will resprout with increased vigor in the spring.

Covering the bushes with a fluffy mulch of oak leaves or straw will serve as sufficient protection through most regions of the country. In fact, our mini roses in a southern New York garden survive winter after winter with nothing but a 6 to 8-inch layer of oak leaves. Any sort of protection that holds in too much heat can prompt growth before spring really arrives.

New growth on 'Baby Darling' will bloom if the fall is long and warm; otherwise, late-fall growth will eventually die during cold winters.

This is why I do not recommend bottles or plastic bag covers in freezing areas.

Hilling

The practice of hilling soil around the base of roses just before the ground freezes in the late fall has real merit. Miniatures will not have to be buried but only covered at the base for 3 to 4 inches. This soil acts as a buffer to prevent stem injury when temperatures fluctuate quickly during winter thaws. Earth around the bush base also protects tissues from winter sunburn and nibbling animals.

When a winter is so harsh that tops are killed, there will be enough live wood with healthy buds below the soil mound to save the plant. When spring has settled and buds begin to swell, gently wash away the soil over a period of a week or so. If your spring rains are heavy, you may even be able to avoid hosing down the soil mounds.

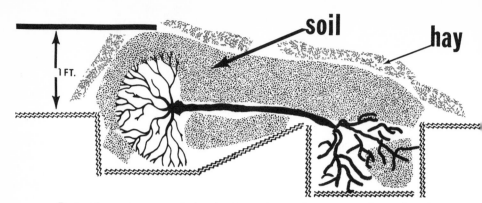

soil

hay

1 FT.

Protect larger tree roses in harsh winter climates by covering the graft and stem with soil. Smaller tree roses can be brought indoors if the winters are severe.

Compost

Use rich compost or topsoil as hilling material. In the Southeast or similar alkaline areas you can mix in 50 percent rough peat moss with the winter hilling soil. This will improve soil by adding organic matter, and the next year soil will be slightly more acid thanks to the peat moss.

One caution about peat moss: avoid using it alone for a mulch or hilling. When peat moss is dry, it sheds water. Only the new chunk-style peat moss materials sold specifically for mulch will permit enough rain to reach the rose roots. Even though tops may not be growing fast in the winter, roots must still be kept evenly moist.

Snow

Snow is an excellent winter cover for miniature roses. If your garden is traditionally covered with a foot or two of snow each winter, the minis should survive perfectly with nothing more than a light leaf mulch. Without snow minis may experience stem injury if the weather goes from warm to cold very quickly, especially if there are strong winds and bright sun.

If these factors occur in your growing region, provide a leaf or straw cover, or protect the bushes with evergreen branches after the Christmas holidays. The needles that fall with warm spring days will provide a delightfully fragrant acid mulch around the roses. For those few gardeners who have overwhelming problems with mice, the best winter protection is still soil around the plant. Straw and evergreen branches give mice places to hide and breed.

Snow is an excellent winter cover for mini roses.

INHERITED HARDINESS

Cold Hardiness

Modern hybridizers are concerned with breeding cold hardiness into their roses. Ernest Williams wrote me that "Hardiness, both cold and heat, is now a must if a variety is to be of more than regional interest. Our plants go to Hawaii, Canada, Alaska, Mexico, England, New Zealand, and Australia as well as all continental states."

Reimer Kordes, famous German hybridizer of W. Kordes Sons, wrote me that their important breeding goals are ". . . to have better plants, larger flowers, and more hardiness. . . . we have lots of crosses with wild forms, just to get more healthiness in the roses." The new Kordes mini pink 'Bonny' is living proof that these desirable traits are being concentrated on in recent releases.

Lyndon Lyon, well-known gesneriad breeder now working with miniature roses, writes: "By winter hardiness we mean plants that need no winter protection and do not freeze back to the ground under our conditions when the temperature goes to 20 and 30 below zero every winter." Since Lyon lives in the chilly Adirondack Mountains of northern New York, his new hybrids will certainly need inherited cold resistance.

Heat Tolerance

Miniatures in my garden have survived many summer heat waves; but the flowers sometimes change color with extreme heat, usually to a faded or less intense shade. Hybridizer Ralph Moore from sunny California and Ernest Williams in Dallas, Texas, both strive for heat resistance in their breeding.

Among more than 200 miniature roses commonly grown, some have been reported as especially rewarding even in continually warm regions.

For example, members of five rose societies near Tampa, Florida, cooperated in a survey published by the Bradenton Rose Society, listing the best roses for Florida gardens. The miniatures recommended included 'Bo-Peep', 'Cinderella', 'June Time', 'Scarlet Gem', and 'Yellow Doll'. All of these hybrids are also thriving in my southern New York garden, a fine testament to the adaptability of miniature roses.

Miniatures grown where frost seldom occurs have a longer season and thus grow taller each year than the same hybrids in colder climates. Also they do not suffer any winter dieback and thus produce a taller bush unless more drastic pruning is done. To keep miniatures low in warm climates, prune hard just before the coolest time of year, or the dry season, whichever is the most dramatic climactic change.

For example, in southern California the minis are cut back in late January or February, then by early spring they have made new growth and begun to bloom. Roses in northern Florida are pruned once each year, in December or January. In warmer southern Florida they may need pruning again by late summer, unless additional height is desired.

A table prepared for a University of Florida Agricultural Extension Service circular lists average heights for miniature roses given good culture in Florida gardens:

'Bo-Peep'	20 inches
'Chipper'	24 inches
'Crici'	30 inches
'Dwarfking'	24 inches

'Jackie'	18 inches
'June Time'	30 inches
"Little Buckaroo'	30 inches
'Pink Cameo'	60 inches (a climber)
'Scarlet Gem'	24 inches
'Starina'	18 inches
'Toy Clown'	18 inches
'Yellow Doll'	18 inches

Why a Cool Rest?

If miniature roses live and bloom for years in climates where frost seldom occurs, why do I recommend a cool rest for indoor-grown bushes? Actually indoor-grown roses will live and bloom without a cool 6 to 8-week minimum dormancy in late fall and winter. However, the indoor display is more dramatic and the bushes easier to keep compact with a dormant period just before indoor forcing.

I say *"forcing"* because these roses are bred from temperate zone species adapted to an annual dormant period. Making the roses grow during cold months is forcing the bushes to produce flowering growths when they would normally be resting, thanks to cool outdoor temperatures, especially at night.

One reason roses can continue year after year in warm climates is that the nights are often cool. With indoor culture the daytime temperatures may match California or Florida, but the night temperatures indoors are consistently above 60°F. Winter night temperatures in Florida and California often drop below 60°F.

Cool Rest Methods

The refrigerator method mentioned previously is practical for a small quantity of bushes, especially well-trimmed plants received in their own small pots from mail order nurseries. For bushes dug up from outdoors or new roses received in full leaf after the growing season, I prefer to rest the potted shrubs outdoors.

In October, over much of the temperate region, new growth above ground will have stopped, but the climate is still mild enough to encourage sturdy new roots. This is an ideal season to pot miniatures for indoor growing. Select containers and soils according to suggestions in chapter 12, then pot each plant while days are still mild.

Water newly potted bushes with a solution of weak low-nitrogen fertilizer and a root stimulant such as Super Thrive (liquid), Transplantone (powder), or Ortho Up-Start (liquid fertilizer plus root stimulant). At this time I also add a teaspoon of Green Garde iron to the solution, to prevent iron chlorosis. Set the pots in a cold frame if you have one available, but keep the top open so bushes do not start new top growth.

I place newly potted minis on a raised bench outdoors rather than in a cold frame. However, because they are so exposed, I must cover them with hay or leaves in late November or move them against a warm house wall once nights start to have hard frosts.

A convenient method is to set all of the pots in flats so that you can move a dozen or so at once. Keep the soil moist and cover the root zone with moist sand or peat moss when temperatures begin to drop below 32°F.

An inexpensive makeshift cold frame can be fashioned from a big crate that has had the bottom replaced with plastic film or an old storm window. This improvised frame will let light in but protect bushes from hard freezing and drying winds, at least through the early winter.

If you want to leave bushes outside after the ground freezes, bury the pots in sand or peat moss and cover the plant tops with several inches of salt hay. Even if the peat moss freezes partially, you will be able to get pots free for the indoor transfer.

Usually you will want to bring the roses indoors by December. The first flush of flowers will appear in 6 to 8 weeks from the time bushes start into growth. If your mini roses will be grown among other houseplants, be on the lookout for pests that may come in from the garden with the roses.

I prefer to protect both the roses and companion plants by spraying with an all-purpose insecticide and fungicide combination an hour or so before the plants are transferred indoors. If it is too cold for spraying outdoors, you can spray in a well-ventilated garage or cellar. An alternative to spraying is a granular systemic applied to the soil (see chapter 17) and weekly foliage showers to keep away pests.

10
Why Spray?

To spray or not to spray is a personal decision. Mini roses *can* be grown without the aid of insecticides. Most certainly your roses can be protected from weeds without herbicides. However there is a but. . . .

Your garden harbors an incredible assortment of organisms, ranging from microscopic bacteria and fungi to vigorous wild plants. Perhaps your neighborhood is plagued with Japanese beetles, whitefly, or aphids. These insects chew plant parts or suck sap for nourishment.

If you are unwilling to give insects part of a rose crop or to have less than perfect flowers, you must protect your plants from natural pests. No organism is inherently harmful or bad biologically. Only when some organism interferes with our specialized human goals do we label it harmful. Similarly, many lovely wild plants become weeds when they grow where we do not want them.

Here are three general approaches to disease and pest control: (1) the 100 percent no-spray way; (2) limited use of sprays for specific problems; or (3) an intensive preventative spray program.

THE NATURAL WAY

The 100 percent no-spray way is the most natural but remember that nature's balance is automatically upset already when you alter the ecology by creating a garden. Clearing land of "weeds" (plants you don't want) to cultivate species you *do* want changes the natural balance and makes your human activity the dominant feature in the garden ecology. Further alteration occurs when exotic insects or diseases are introduced.

The Japanese beetle did not evolve in the United States. This pest is an Asian insect that was accidentally introduced into our country. Other exotic troubles include some virus strains and numerous plants we call weeds.

These organisms are new to your garden, but so are most of the plants you want to grow. Ecologists have long recognized that control of any organism is a complex process. Simply killing off one species will often not achieve a desired goal, at least not for long.

Pest control is complex because organisms interact. Living forms exist in a web of intricate relationships, many of which we still do not completely understand.

What does this mean in your garden? A practical approach to pest control involves both pest control and optimum plant culture. By growing sturdy bushes you make it harder for pests to seriously damage or kill them. If you would like to minimize or even eliminate the use of chemical sprays in your garden, you must understand how this can be done as well as what is likely to occur.

Compromise

For the 100 percent no-spray approach, be willing to compromise crop quality. Very few gardens can be kept pest free, even with insecticides. If you choose not to spray, then some of your roses will be partially damaged.

A few buds may be eaten, some foliage will be lost to black spot fungus or mildew, a few more minutes will be needed to pull weeds. But some good things will happen too.

Benefits

By eliminating chemical sprays in the garden you provide a more favorable environment for useful insects. Birds will be encouraged to help with pest control too, especially if you set up a small pool for drinking and bathing (just a hose trickling into a pan will do).

You will reduce garden expenses by saving money on pesticides, herbicides, sprayers, and labor. Your health may also be better. Even when carefully applied, pesticides present some hazard to health. As an overall approach to gardening, the organic way has many advantages and only a few disadvantages.

MODIFIED SPRAY PROGRAM

The second approach to pest and disease control incorporates the cultural practices of a 100 percent natural system with limited spraying. Insecticides are applied only when specific pests begin doing damage. If you favor this approach, choose a spray to control the specific pests or diseases on your roses. Apply the product according to package directions, never in stronger concentrations.

Procedures

Some practical methods for controlling pests, weeds, and disease without chemical sprays include:

1. Prepare soil carefully, mixing in peat moss and humus according to suggestions in chapter 5.

Wash foliage with warm water to keep insect pests under control and to wash dust away from leaves on indoor roses. Bushes at right wait for their shower in a Plexite waterproof saucer, sold with three wheels as a caster for large indoor plants but also useful to hold several smaller pots.

2. Mulch to control weeds, conserve moisture, reduce spread of fungus spores, and increase soil humus.

3. Water when required and soak ground for deep root systems.

4. Space roses to provide room for growth, reduce root competition, and increase air circulation.

5. Cultivate useful companion plants. For example, dwarf marigolds deter nematodes. In the fall cut marigolds off at soil level, compost tops, and let the roots rot in the garden.

6. Insure that your roses will get maximum sun. Sun encourages sturdy growth and optimum flowering.

7. Support trailing or climbing types to maintain air circulation and control their growth style.

8. Fertilize roses during the growing season (see chapter 6).

9. Wash foliage with a strong stream from the hose at least once a week. Washing off plants, especially the undersides of foliage, will control spider mites and aphids. Morning or midafternoon are good times to hose down mini rosebushes. They should be dry by dark. Avoid a very cold water bath to foliage when sun is hot, such as at midday. Washing foliage is good for indoor roses too.

10. Welcome helpful creatures who will control many garden pests.

Predators and Parasites

Useful predators and parasites are of considerable economic and aesthetic benefit in your garden. You will have hours of pleasure watching birds and listening to their songs. These beautiful creatures will also eat quantities of harmful insects. Less lovely but still fascinating to watch are praying mantids and ladybugs, useful insects that prey on harmful insects. Parasites are not much fun to think about, but if they infest harmful insects you will benefit from their parasitic action. Some useful natural predators and parasites around roses include:

Birds—Attract them with food and water. Even with a supplement of grain, suet, and bread, the birds will kill an incredible quantity of pests. Parent songbirds feed their young with soft-bodied insects.

Ladybugs—Although harmless to humans, the red and black ladybugs (species of *Hippodamia*) are dangerous predators to aphids and mealybugs. One ladybug larva can consume 40 aphids per day. If your garden has few ladybugs, you can import a box of live *H. convergens* each spring to help control pests (chapter 19 lists sources).

This friendly ladybug hunts aphids on one of my mini roses.

A helpful praying mantis is searching for pests on a bush of 'Popcorn'.

Praying Mantids—A praying mantis may look frightening, but except for its ability to scratch, it is harmless to us. Mantids are carnivorous creatures and will kill many of the larger insect pests. I have seen mantids catch butterflies, seemingly inoffensive and beautiful insects but nevertheless only recently transformed from pesty caterpillars. To increase the mantid population in your garden, tie egg masses (sold as clusters) to the larger rosebushes in early spring. When warm weather arrives, a swarm of 100 to 200 young mantids will hatch out of each egg mass. Even after eating each other there will still be some left to grow fat on harmful insects.

Two biological controls currently being used in England and being tested in the United States are a red spider mite predator, *Phytoseiulus persimilis*, and *Encarsia formosa*, a parasite of the whitefly insect. The Royal Horticultural Society offers supplies of these useful biological controls to members in England, but so far I have not located a source in the United States. Perhaps by the time you read this these useful creatures will be commercially available in the United States.

Nonvenomous snakes should be welcome in every garden. A 12-inch DeKay snake lives in my garden between a bush of 'White Gem' and a dwarf mugho pine. It is startling to come upon this small creature, but I know it helps keep the roses free from pests. Black snakes and similar species like the garter snakes may eat some useful earthworms but they also eat quite a few insects. King snakes are not too useful for insect control, but they will eat rattlesnakes.

By eating a constant succession of insects, the common toad is of immense benefit in any garden. Toads will be encouraged to live in your garden if they can find some water nearby. Even a shallow 1 to 2-inch deep pool, kept filled with a trickling hose, will please them. Gardens near streams, ponds, or a marsh usually have both toads and frogs. The terrestrial toads are more helpful than the nearly entirely aquatic frogs.

Useful Microbes

Some natural control of pests can be achieved by microbes that cause pests to become diseased. The most useful for rose culture is an organism that causes the milky disease of Japanese beetle grubs (*Popilla japonica*). The adult form of Japanese beetles eat flowers, and the grub form destroys roots.

When grubs are infected with milky-disease bacterium, they soon die. Spores of the disease organism remain in the soil to infect future grubs. In a few years the milky disease will kill off most of the Japanese beetles in a given area.

The commercially available form of milky-disease spore powder is called Doom (Fairfax Biological Laboratory). I tried this in my garden ten years ago and have only recently begun to see an occasional Japanese beetle. Of course, the pests gradually develop an immunity, or at least a resistance, to many diseases, as they do to most insecticides. But this biological control is still quite effective and not dangerous.

Bacillus thuringiensis is a bacterium that helps control bagworms, webworms, and certain other chewing insects but does not harm warm-blooded animals or bees. The bacteria are sold as Thuricide, Biotol, and Dipel. Insects that eat leaves or buds sprayed with this bacterial insecticide develop paralysis of the digestive tract and soon perish.

Limited Spraying

Apply most of the techniques favored for the natural control methods outlined above and you will have a lovely crop of roses. In fact your garden in general will be peaceful and healthy.

However, calamity can come to Eden. Since the garden has an inherently artificial ecology, certain pests or diseases may, from time to time, become overabundant. If this happens in your garden, a modified spray program will protect the status quo.

DIAGNOSIS

Step one in the treatment is diagnosis. Apply no spray until you have identified the pest or disease. By using specific chemicals designed to control certain organisms, you will protect many useful insects, reduce health hazards, and save money.

See chapter 17 for details about common miniature rose pests and diseases. Consult local agricultural extension agents, university horticultural departments, and botanical gardens for help with puzzling problems.

The more experienced members of the American Rose Society are identified as consulting rosarians. In every region their responsibility to this title is to help gardeners by providing personalized rose culture advice without charge. Your local chapter of the A.R.S. can put you in touch with consulting rosarians who are able to advise which chemicals do the most effective job in your region.

RESTRAINED APPLICATION AND PRECISE PREPARATION

Once you diagnose the problem and obtain an effective remedy, apply the spray with restraint. Treat plants that require it, but avoid massive spraying of your whole garden just to control aphids on a few roses. Remember that we are talking of a *modified* spray program.

Mix each chemical according to package directions or precise instructions from a plant pathologist. Chemical companies, encouraged by increasingly strict laws, spend millions of dollars developing and testing agricultural sprays. The final recommendations listed on each product label are based on careful testing. Using a lesser concentration or application may fail to control the problem. A greater concentration or application often harms plants, the environment, and certainly costs more money. Correctly mixed, carefully applied sprays are helpful and relatively safe.

GRANULAR SYSTEMICS

Some modern pesticides are available in dry granular form. The granules release a poison that is absorbed in solution by the roots and distributed throughout the plant. Sucking and chewing pests are poisoned when they attack the rose. Ortho Rose and Flower Care is one systemic specifically formulated for roses. The Ortho products include an 8-12-4 fertilizer.

SANITATION

Keeping your garden 100 percent free from disease and pests is impossible with a modified spray program and organic culture. By definition the natural method of cultivation includes an organic mulch. Still you *will* help stop problems by reducing the accumulation of diseased parts.

For example, rose leaves infected with black spot fungus or powdery mildew should be thrown into the garbage. Stems with disease belong in the trash, not the compost pile. This is easier to do in small gardens or with roses in containers, but even a semimonthly garden bed cleanup of diseased parts helps.

PREVENTATIVE SPRAYING

Gardeners eager to win top prizes at shows are most likely to need a week-to-week spray program because of the increased susceptibility of some modern hybrids to mildew and the inherent nature of show judging, which puts emphasis on "perfection."

Fortunately miniature roses are easier to keep healthy than larger hybrid teas or floribundas. Minis require less spray, and with careful selection you can obtain hybrids genetically resistant to fungus. If you decide to apply a complete preventative spray program, your work begins in the early spring (or just after midwinter pruning in warm regions).

Combining Materials

Study product labels to determine which chemicals can be combined. With all-purpose rose sprays this is hardly a problem, since the combination has already been made, but you may want to customize your spray materials. A widely used rose spray combination is Isotox insecticide (1 tablespoon per gallon) with Phaltan fungicide (1 tablespoon per gallon). Insects and disease are controlled with the same spray.

Most water-soluble fertilizers can also be effectively combined with fungicides and insecticides. By adding ½ tablespoon of Peters 18-18-18 or Miracle Gro to each gallon of the Isotox/Phaltan or Isotox/Benlate spray, you formulate a triple-purpose spray. Healthy, well-nourished roses resist disease better than weak bushes.

Spraying Frequency

If black spot is a primary problem, apply fungicide after every rain and whenever you find evidence of infection. For powdery mildew the spray must be applied before mildew starts, then every 8 to 10 days during the growing season.

For maximum preventative control, insecticides should be applied just before growth begins in the spring, and then every 8 to 10 days during the growing season.

When this sort of preventative spray program is combined with optimum culture of top hybrids, you will have outstanding roses, sure to win prizes.

Spraying Techniques

How a spray is applied influences its effectiveness. The most potent preparations will not act efficiently if they fail to reach pests or diseased tissues. I find the modern sprayers helpful for applying sprays efficiently. Two of my favorites have nozzles that can direct spray streams precisely where I want, even to the undersides of the foliage on short miniatures.

For example, the portable Hudson Cordless sprayer has an attached extension tube behind the stream-to-mist nozzle. The tube can bend down at one end, then up at the other, and the nozzle is also on a swivel. Spray can

The Hudson Cordless electric sprayer has an adjustable nozzle so spray can reach undersides of leaves.

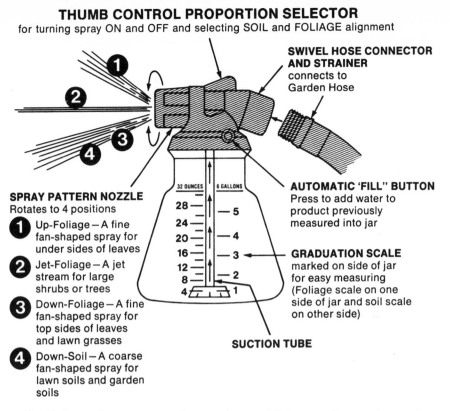

THUMB CONTROL PROPORTION SELECTOR

for turning spray ON and OFF and selecting SOIL and FOLIAGE alignment

SWIVEL HOSE CONNECTOR AND STRAINER
connects to
Garden Hose

SPRAY PATTERN NOZZLE
Rotates to 4 positions

1 Up-Foliage – A fine fan-shaped spray for under sides of leaves

2 Jet-Foliage – A jet stream for large shrubs or trees

3 Down-Foliage – A fine fan-shaped spray for top sides of leaves and lawn grasses

4 Down-Soil – A coarse fan-shaped spray for lawn soils and garden soils

AUTOMATIC 'FILL" BUTTON
Press to add water to product previously measured into jar

GRADUATION SCALE
marked on side of jar for easy measuring (Foliage scale on one side of jar and soil scale on other side)

SUCTION TUBE

The Ortho garden sprayer attaches to a hose and has many directional controls. (Drawing courtesy of Chevron Chemical Co.)

thus be directed from below a bush. This is a useful sprayer for misting indoor plants too.

Another type of sprayer that has many spray directions, at the flip of a wheel, is Ortho's garden sprayer. This is a proportioner device that attaches to a hose. It mixes a concentrated solution with hose water in a precise proportion but must remain attached to a hose while in operation.

For limited applications of spray, often required for indoor roses, the small quart to half-gallon plastic misters are useful but they do not last long. Sprayers of all types should be flushed with clean warm water after every chemical application.

Dust

Some pesticides and fungicides are available as dust, designed to be applied dry directly to foliage. Portable dusters, offered in several rose catalogs, are practical and easy to use.

Rose dust sticks to foliage and flowers, thus providing effective action. However, the dust is highly visible. Compared with the almost invisible residue of liquid sprays, dust is definitely unsightly. The few times I have used dust, just to test its effectiveness, the roses looked so messy that I have switched to water-based materials. My objection to dusting is aesthetic, since in some cases the dust is slightly more effective and longer lasting than liquid sprays. However, for thorough coverage on all foliage surfaces a fine wet mist is better.

PART III

INDOOR CULTURE

Miniature roses grow just outside this kitchen window and thus provide a constant growing-season show without any indoor care. Herbs and cactus grow indoors. During the winter potted miniature roses can be grown alongside these kitchen plants.

11
The Indoor Environment

Miniature roses do make delightful houseplants. With a basic understanding of their simple requirements you can have roses every day from late fall to spring, or all year long if you wish.

Some indoor gardeners will challenge my enthusiasm for miniature roses as houseplants. These readers have had a brief experience with minis indoors and invariably tell me that their indoor roses failed because "red spider mites took over" or "flowers were too sparse." Both of these common problems can be solved with good horticultural practices.

In my collection red spider mites are controlled with water washes, limited spraying with miticides, and strict quarantine of new plants that may introduce these tenacious pests. Spider mites can be controlled, and you can have healthy roses indoors.

Those well-grown mini roses that fail to flower freely are starved for light. By providing broad-spectrum fluorescent lamps (see chapter 13) or by growing plants in a sunny south or west window, you will have roses all winter long. Select some modern hybrids that have a constant blooming habit (see chapters 3 and 4).

CIRCULATION AND HUMIDITY

For healthy foliage and lasting flowers the air must be moist. A relative humidity of 40 percent is satisfactory, but 50 to 60 percent is better. Mini roses in my basement have 60 percent humidity. When the air is moist, pests such as spider mites are discouraged. Bushes are free to grow normally, without dropping an excessive number of leaves or producing small, short-lived flowers.

Air should also be fresh and moving. In plant rooms, light gardens, and basements install a fan to run 24 hours per day. The fan will help stop mildew and black spot. Moving air is especially important when humidity is high or bushes are touching each other.

In living areas a constantly running fan may not be acceptable, except during warm months. Provide air circulation by leaving a window partially open in mild weather. When it is cold outside, leave doors open to adjoining rooms. Neither people nor roses thrive with stale air.

Provide humid air by growing roses over trays of water or moist material such as gravel or perlite. You may already be using this technique for other houseplants.

Fill a metal or plastic tray with gravel or perlite, then add water and keep the filling moist. Place rose pots on plastic wedged-louver sections or inverted clay saucers on top of the moist tray filling.

Rose pots placed directly on the moist filling will soon be hard to move because roots will have grown out of the bottom. An efficient way to provide humidity but prevent root escape is to put wooden, plastic, or wire

'Baby Betsy McCall' escaped out the drainage holes and developed an extensive hydroponic root system in the water inside the outer decorative container. This growth pattern is similar to that found with the wick-watering pots used with other indoor plants.

grids completely over a water-filled tray. I use this technique for roses under lights.

Placing mini roses among companion houseplants, or grouping the bushes, will help maintain a humid microclimate. Groups of plants, by releasing water through leaf pores (stomata), aid one another and form a favorable environment, a factor not occurring around isolated plants.

Misting

It does help to lightly mist roses with warm water during the day. A plain water mist discourages spider mites, raises humidity, and washes away accumulated dust. Keep a plastic spray bottle filled with plain water near windowsill-grown roses.

Several times each day as you pass by, mist the foliage, an easy chore because you will be looking over your plants anyway. The main precaution with misting is to let foliage dry before nightfall. If any plants develop black spot fungus, suspend misting until the disease is controlled.

A precision hygrometer will show you if humidity is adequate for healthy rose growth.

Humidifiers

In situations where room humidity is drastically low, a mechanical humidifier is useful, perhaps required. The larger electrically operated console models of 6-gallon capacity or more are most practical. Smaller units have to be filled too often in dry weather. Even easier to use, but harder to install, are humidifiers that attach to the waterline.

The Hermidifier is one excellent unit of this type that sends out a fog by centrifugal action. The fog appears whenever the unit is activated by an attached humistat. However, the Hermidifier and similar units are only practical in larger rooms, basements, and greenhouses. For windowsill gardens, living rooms, and similar situations the plug-in portable humidifiers are satisfactory, even though they must be manually filled.

TEMPERATURE

Miniature-rose flowers last longest when temperatures are 45° to 55°F., and plants grow most slowly at these temperatures. Few of us can provide these low temperatures indoors. Even if we could, the roses would grow much too slowly for maximum flower production. Therefore I recommend a 60° to 65°F. minimum night temperature. The countless minis I have grown indoors do perfectly with this range.

Your indoor roses will make sturdy growth with the 60° to 65°F. nights. Daytime temperatures into the high 70's are perfectly satisfactory when you provide the bushes with adequate light. Humidity, temperature, and light work in concert. When they are balanced correctly, houseplants thrive.

Results are poor when high temperatures are combined with low light levels, since warmer temperatures encourage rapid growth, but without bright light the stems will be weak. Low humidity is especially harmful when light is hot and bright. Moderate temperatures between 60° and 75°F., 50 percent humidity, and bright light form the optimum environment for indoor roses.

A maximum-minimum thermometer gives precise information on the highest and lowest temperatures in any area.

LIGHT

Your roses will have the most floriferous compact growth and richest color when given strong light. Miniatures may look delicate, but remember that outdoors they thrive in full sun. Indoors, roses will still grow with less light, but flowering decreases as light levels drop.

Place roses at south or west windows where the sun is not blocked by nearby buildings or trees. Give them as much sun as possible or supplement sun with fluorescents if necessary. I have grown miniature roses in cool north windows to study their reaction. These plants did flower, but the blooms were less numerous and the colors somewhat lighter than normal for the variety. Also, roses with weak light made spindly stems. If you have only a dim window for roses, you can improve conditions by adding broad-spectrum fluorescent lamps above or alongside the roses (see chapter 13 for details about artificial light).

MICROCLIMATES

Obtain a maximum-minimum thermometer to determine the temperature range in all possible rose growing areas. Many homes have some windows or corner rooms where temperatures are several degrees lower than elsewhere in the house.

Apartment dwellers usually find somewhat less variation, but unless radiators are under windows the glassed areas are usually cooler. When you have a choice, grow roses where nights are coolest, all other factors being equal. Consistently warm indoor nights encourage rapid growth and short-lived flowers, the same as with outdoor roses during hot summers.

Roses I grow in the living room, along the sills of south to west windows, have a 63° to 65°F. night range in the winter. They are sturdy and bloom throughout the winter. It is a special treat to have fragrant miniature roses in flower on the windowsill, while outside the ground is covered with snow.

12
Containers
and Soils

Miniature roses will grow in a wide range of pots if you furnish good drainage. Under no circumstances do I recommend using nondrained containers, except as decorative cover for drained pots. For a collection of special roses indoors I like to use many different container styles, to fit the pot to each hybrid. Less expensive and somewhat easier to care for are groups of plants in the same size and style of container.

HARD PLASTIC

Pots of shiny plastic loose water only through drainage holes. No water evaporates through pot walls, so soil dries out slowly. Most of my miniature roses under lights in the basement are growing in shiny plastic. Especially attractive are new pot styles with decorative contours such as the Carefree Deco Pots in white, yellow, red, or black. Although square plastic pots allow room for more pots per square foot than round pots, this is advantageous only for small plants, since the pots will have to be spaced as the bushes grow.

The large garden centers typically offer shelves and shelves of different containers. Besides being sure of basically intelligent design features such as adequate drainage and suitable size, you can choose colors or designs to suit your taste. Among the plastic pots nationally available are some extra-heavy-grade plastic types, such as Plexite pots that come with snap-on saucers. There is a clear and a slightly smoked Plexite pot that lets you see soil, a great help when you need to learn about watering. I think it's fun to watch new roots develop too.

Containers for miniature roses include these attractive pots from different sources. *Top left,* plastic Cherokee basket with built-in saucer, smokey-clear Plexite pot, and rustic cork planter; *front,* daisy-decorated clear plastic pot by Plexite, square 4½-inch plastic pot in green, clear Plexite pot with clip-on saucer, and plastic Lockwood basket with built-in saucer; *lower right,* a small plastic pot used by mini rose growers for plants mailed out to consumers. Rose 'Pearl Dawn' is at left, 'Green Ice' in the center.

FOAM PLASTIC

Styrofoam plastic containers, offered as Tufflite and Poly-Pots, do lose water through pot walls. Although foam pots dry out more slowly than plain clay, they still permit an air exchange around roots. This is an advantage if you are a chronic overwaterer or use a very heavy potting mix. Some growers like the matte finish and rough texture of foam pots more than the glossy plastic types. The foam pots come in white, terra cotta color, and a simulated wood-grain finish.

CLAY

Standard clay pots are satisfactory for roses but only if you pay strict attention to regular watering. Unglazed clay dries out very quickly, especially around established roses that have filled the pot with roots. However, the clay's porosity encourages healthy white roots and is the best material for pots that will be sunk outdoors in soil or peat for the summer.

Glazed clay may behave like shiny plastic if fully coated, or like the foam pots if only partially glazed. One style I find well suited to miniature roses is the bonsai pot. These come in various shapes from square through oblong, quite shallow to tall and deep.

Smaller 2 to 3-inch bonsai pots are suitable for micro minis or seedlings. I have a 3-inch tall plant of yellow-flowered 'Littlest Angel' in a low square blue-glazed bonsai pot, truly charming under lights. Larger minis grow best in 4 to 6-inch bonsai pots. The deep style offers good root space.

I like brilliantly colored hybrids in the subdued plain earth-brown pots. Single-flowered miniatures such as 'Simplex', 'Peachy White', and 'Kara' look nice in pots partially decorated with glaze or inscribed with simple white Oriental drawings against dark clay. Most bonsai pots come with matching saucers.

Roses that have extensive roots, like this bush of 'Rouletii', should be repotted at once. This plant will be potted in a foam-plastic container.

The bottom of this root ball will be slightly pulled apart to encourage new feeder roots.

CORK AND WOOD

Although less lasting than other container materials, wood and cork are suitable for baskets, boxes, and pots. I have some planters fashioned from Portuguese cork. The bottoms are of pressed wood material protected with a resin coating like fiberglass. Some cork pots are naturally decorated with green or yellow lichens that dry out but remain attached once the bark has been removed from the cork oak tree.

The imported cork (Portuguese and Spanish) is expensive. To make cork planters last, they can be lined with plastic or used just to display roses actually grown in other containers. For example, I display some flowering roses from my basement light garden by setting the 4-inch plastic pots inside a larger decorative cork tub.

Wooden pots and baskets fashioned from cypress or redwood will last for several years, even with soil placed directly against the wood. For the

Lyndon Lyon's #P-16, a watermelon-red mini under testing, grows well in a glazed but drained container. Fir bark is used as a mulch for this specimen grown under fluorescent lights.

longest service from wooden containers, paint them first with Cuprinol wood preservative. Allow the containers to dry for 2 days and rinse them briefly before using.

BASKETS

The most practical baskets for indoor use have built-in or clip-on saucers. With an attached saucer you can water hanging baskets with

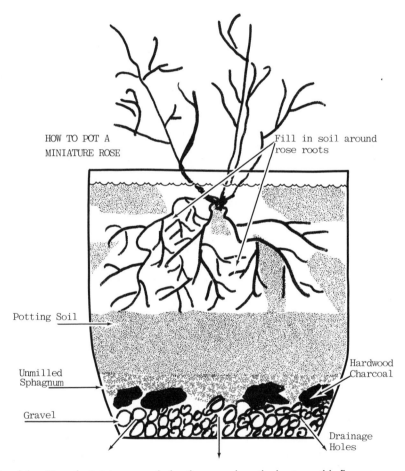

HOW TO POT A
MINIATURE ROSE

Fill in soil around
rose roots

Potting Soil

Unmilled
Sphagnum

Hardwood
Charcoal

Gravel

Drainage
Holes

Careful potting of miniature roses helps them produce the best possible flowers.

reduced risk of soaking rugs and furniture. Outdoors, baskets without saucers are suitable.

Plastic baskets with adjustable metal wire hangers are efficient and long lasting. Some of the better modern types are quite tough and will not shatter or crack if dropped. Nationally available baskets offered in garden stores and by mail-order include one by Plexite with a removable saucer and a built-in white nylon cord for hanging. The 6 to 8-inch sizes are best for trailing mini roses but use the larger sizes of 10 to 12 inches if you have space for plants to develop indoors.

POT SIZES

Mini roses adapt well to small pots if moisture is evenly maintained. They do not prosper if given too large a pot because the soil mix usually stays soggy. Small to medium-sized pots, 3 to 6 inches, soon fill with vigorous, firm roots, and soil water is absorbed quickly.

Propagations grow well for a year in 3-inch pots, but they bush out faster if given 4 to 5-inch pots once roots are seen at the drainage holes of the smaller pots. Commercial growers often ship miniature roses in deep narrow plastic pots 2½ to 3 inches across. These are good for rooting cuttings later, so save them even if you transplant the new roses to larger containers.

SOIL MIXTURES

An excellent uniform potting mix made from easily available pest-free materials is:

6 parts coarse sphagnum peat moss

3 parts coarse perlite

3 parts horticultural vermiculite

Dusting of dolomite limestone

Combine the ingredients in a large container—a clean wheelbarrow or big heavy-duty plastic bag—and mix thoroughly. This peat-base mix will promote excellent root growth and is similar to commercially offered peat-base formulas such as Jiffy-Mix, Pro-Mix, and other soil-free potting soils. Store these mixes dry, then moisten slightly if they are very dry at potting time.

Useful materials for rose potting soils and outdoor soil modification include vermiculite, prepared rosebush potting soils, or commercial peat-lite mixes, perlite, Viterra hydrogel to hold more moisture in the mix, and rough sphagnum peat moss. The rose is light yellow 'Little Linda'.

Ingredients for indoor soil mixes should be prepared in clean containers, uncontaminated with outdoor earth.

The W. R. Grace Company offers a potting soil specifically designed for roses, Terra-Lite Rose Bush Planting Soil. The mixture has a slight quantity of slow-release fertilizer (Mag Amp) and is balanced to provide the best pH for roses. Since the fertilizer is added to the vermiculite in very low concentrations, you must fertilize potted roses after several weeks once roots are firmly established.

I add slow-release fertilizers to soil-free potting mixes to assure a steady supply of nutrients. Some, like Mag Amp, are designed to be blended into the soil, while others direct that the granules be placed on top of the soil. Follow package directions of whichever product you use.

Osmocote 14-14-14, Precise Rose Formula 8-12-4, and Ortho 5-10-5 Pot and Planter Food timed release granules are slow-release fertilizers designed to be sprinkled over the soil surface. With every watering a minute quantity of fertilizer is released into the root zone. In addition to the major ingredients of nitrogen, phosphorus, and potassium these fertilizers provide trace elements or micronutrients. During the most active growing period I supplement these chemical formulas with monthly applications of seaweed and fish emulsion fertilizers.

A primary advantage of packaged commercial mixes, or your own mixture based on clean packaged materials, is that no pests are introduced. Plain garden soil, unless pasteurized, contains pests and disease spores that cause problems indoors. Using a commercially prepared formula further offers a uniform mixture with consistent quality. Once you master culture with a certain brand, you can count on future bags of the same mix giving repeatable results.

Should you prefer to use a heavier mix with actual soil, thus reducing the need for constant fertilizing, add ⅓ to ½ pasteurized soil by volume to the peat-base mix. Where shipping distance is not too great, it is practical to buy potting mixtures from mini rose specialists. Nor' East Miniature Roses, for example, sells their own "Super Soil" formula in sealed plastic bags of 1 or 3 quarts.

HYDROGEL

Established roses in containers may require water everyday in the peat-base mixtures. To reduce watering chores, I add a hydrogel soil amendment to the potting mix. The hydrogel, offered as Viterra by W. Atlee Burpee Company, holds water until required for growth, yet it does not cause air to be driven out of the medium. To determine when a rose needs water (in whatever mix), use pot weight as a quick indication. After a week or so of lifting a dry potted plant, then comparing it with a just watered plant of the same size, you will be able to judge when a rose needs water by just lifting up the pot slightly. Clay pots can also be tested by a slight tap on the side (I use my ring). A hollow sound means water is required, while a dull thud means the soil mix still has plenty of moisture.

POTTING PROCEDURES

Sharp drainage is important, so begin potting with a supply of gravel or broken clay pots (crocks). Place ½ inch of drainage material in the bottom of each container. Next add a few small ½ to 1-inch chunks of hardwood charcoal and a ¼ to ½-inch layer of unmilled sphagnum moss. The hardwood charcoal absorbs noxious gases and chemical salts. Unmilled sphagnum moss prevents the potting mix from filling up the drainage area or running out of the drainage holes.

A newly received bush of 'Angel Darling' will be potted into a clear plastic Plexite pot. First gravel, hardwood charcoal, and unmilled sphagnum moss are placed in the new pot.

'Angel Darling' is removed from the old shipping pot and set in the clip-on saucer supplied with the Plexite pot. The former pot is used to create a correctly shaped hole for the 'Angel Darling' root ball.

The completed repotting job gives 'Angel Darling' room to grow. Now the bush will be watered-in with a transplanting solution. The clear Plexite pot permits you to watch roots grow.

To repot or move roses up to a larger container, first turn the plant up-side down, spreading your fingers over the soil ball, with the stems be-tween your fingers. Knock the pot edge with a trowel or against a firm hard surface such as a potting-table edge. The root ball should come free and release the rose from its old pot.

Spray the exposed root ball with water and set the plant aside (out of the sun if you are working outdoors). Put an inch or more of soil mix into the new pot, then place the old pot inside the new pot, with the rim ½ to 1 inch lower than your larger new pot. Fill in soil all around, packing firmly. Remove the old pot, and the resulting hole will perfectly accept the root ball.

Before setting in the rose, gently pull loose the old drainage material. This will stimulate new roots to form. Drop the rose into the depression, tap the pot sharply on your table to settle soil, then water thoroughly with a transplanting solution.

TRANSPLANTING SOLUTION

Mix a transplanting solution to stimulate new roots and drench each newly potted rose. I use a solution of Transplantone (a powder) or Super Thrive (drops) mixed with a ¼-strength fertilizer solution. A similar stimulant/fertilizer solution offered as a liquid is Ortho Up-Start, a 5-15-5 fertilizer with indole-3-butyric acid. Whichever products you choose, prepare the solution with warm water. In addition to being a weak fertilizer, this solution has hormones that encourage new root growth.

SEEDLINGS AND ROOTED CUTTINGS

Seedlings and recently rooted cuttings seldom have a tight root ball. They require a slightly different potting method than do established, pot-bound roses.

Place a small mound of potting mix in the pot. Spread roots out over the mound and, while supporting the stem with one hand, fill-in around the roots with additional potting mix. Place the plant about ½ inch deeper in the new pot than it had been in the old one, tapping the pot several times to gently settle soil. Soak the soil with transplanting solution. If the potting mix is rather dry, put the newly potted roses in a tray or saucer with about ½ inch of water around the bottom of the pot. Pour off any liquid that has not been absorbed after 3 or 4 hours.

13
Growing
Under Lights

Growing miniature roses under fluorescent lights is efficient, effective, and easy. These tiny shrubs are well suited to light gardens because they flower all year long, have bright colors, many are fragrant, and mini roses are compatible with a wide range of other houseplants.

Mini roses will grow under lights wherever you provide suitable temperatures and humidity. My experiments in growing them under lights prove that even so important a factor as temperature can vary greatly. For example, in a cool studio with winter nights down to 40°F. my mini roses almost stand still. When weather moderates and nights seldom drop below 55°F., the bushes start to grow again.

Daytime temperatures 8 to 10 degrees higher than night lows encourage flowers. Since the room is so cool, flowers last a week or more.

At the other extreme are plants in a warm section of my basement. Roses on the top tier of a light cart have minimum nights around 68°F. So long as I maintain a humidity of 50 to 60 percent (see chapter 11), the bushes thrive. Warm nights encourage fast growth. Thanks to strong broad-spectrum fluorescent lighting, each stem is sturdy and flowering is abundant.

In between the warm location and a chilly room come the average conditions you most likely have in your den, bedroom, and living room, with nights around 65°F. and days into the high 70's, a perfect range for mini roses. Sometimes, as in my collection, these temperatures occur in a basement near the outside wall. Once you determine which area in your home has the best temperatures for roses, plan to install suitable fluorescent fixtures.

I grew these *Rosa chinensis minima* seedlings from seed to flowering in 9 weeks under broad-spectrum fluorescent lights.

FIXTURE SELECTION

Choose the largest possible fixture for the space available. A fixture with four 40-watt lamps (48 inches to 50 inches long) is more efficient than setting two 20-watt fixtures (24 to 26 inches long) end to end. Fluorescent lamps loose intensity at both ends.

Roses are high-light-requirement plants. When they begin to grow, the light must be intense or stems will be weak and flowering poor. Fixtures with four lamps are commonly available, and I find them efficient for roses. While plants are just leafing out, you can switch the units to use only two lamps, then turn on all four when growth is underway.

Fixtures holding only one lamp are of little use for flowering plants. A compromise is fixtures holding two lamps. Where roses receive some daylight, or for display of flowering specimens grown elsewhere, two broad-spectrum lamps hung 3 to 4 inches above foliage are sufficient. However, for maximum efficiency and plant performance install at least a three or four-lamp fixture.

Commercial fixtures offered for light gardens have reflectors of polished aluminum or white enamel. Lamps are spaced differently from fixture to fixture, depending upon the manufacturer, but I find tube type and lamp-to-plant distance more important than slight differences in lamp arrangement. Set the lamps three to four inches apart if you are building your own light garden from scratch.

Aluminum fixtures holding four 40-watt fluorescents help me grow perfect roses in the basement.

Miniature roses can be well grown under a combination of daylight and fluorescent lights. A fixture such as this with two 20-watt tubes will grow fine bushes when lamps are broad-spectrum types and the roses receive some direct sunlight each day. The bushes here are growing in a tray of moist gravel for added humidity. Companion plants tucked between the pots are terrestrial *Cryptanthus* bromeliads. The roses are, *left to right:* 'Plum Cove', 'Little Linda', in a low bonsai pot; 'Mimi', in clear Plexite pot; 'Green Ice', branching over to in front of 'Mimi'; micro-mini 'Littlest Angel', in 3½-inch glazed bonsai dish; 'Pearl Dawn'; and *far right*, 'Seabreeze'.

LIGHT STANDS

Several well-designed light-garden stands are offered nationally and are efficient for roses when ordered with four-lamp fixtures (each holds at least four tubes). I grow roses on an aluminum Flora Cart (Tube Craft Company) and in a tiered light garden of redwood and aluminum designed by the Shoplite Company. Similar stands are offered by several other firms listed in chapter 19. Your choice depends somewhat on aesthetics. A certain design may fit in your living area better than another. Even in my basement I did not like the industrial-looking paint color of some fixtures, but a can of Rust-Oleum metal paint let me change the color quickly.

You can customize the frames and exterior (top) of reflectors to fit any decorating plan. Complete suggestions and many photos are found in my *Complete Book of Houseplants Under Lights* (Hawthorn, 1975).

PORTABLE UNITS

Freestanding fixtures, self-contained wall garden modules, and 22-watt circline units are suitable for displaying roses. The newer portable fixtures (Marko, Shoplite, etc.) that can be ordered in three or four-lamp models are also sufficiently bright to grow roses year after year.

Circline fixtures currently offered for plants come with 22-watt Wide-Spectrum Gro-Lux tubes, an efficient horticultural lamp. If plants receive some sunlight each day, coupled with 14 hours of fluorescent light, even the circline plant fixtures can help you grow sturdy roses.

A main advantage of self-contained, plug-in fixtures is their portability. For more permanent light gardens that must look attractive, a new design by the Marko Company is superior. The Marko lights feature a built-in para-wedge louver shield that hides the lamps. By shielding lamps from view, these wedges prevent glare yet permit almost all of the lamp light to shine directly down on the roses. This is an excellent light garden for decorative installations in bookshelves or against walls in living areas. The wood finish waterproofed Marko garden tray matches the fixture, but the para-wedge lamp fixture can be purchased alone and installed above any sort of shelf, tray, or bench.

BASEMENT FIXTURES

Away from living areas, in spare rooms or basements, fixtures can be more utilitarian. Simple efficiency and low cost are often more important than decorative design. In my basement the roses thrive under shiny aluminum fixtures, each holding four 40-watt lamps.

Galvanized chain hangs the fixtures above plants, with no special installation required except for a few sturdy screw eyes in the wooden joists above. The galvanized chain can be bent apart at any link using a needle-nose pliers. The chain hooks directly into holes that are an integral part of the reflector top. By adjusting the chain, I can quickly set the lamp height. The aluminum fixtures (Shoplite Company) have AC plugs, so one fixture can be plugged into the next. The last unit is plugged into an automatic timer, which you can obtain at hardware stores or the light-garden firms listed in chapter 19.

Roses in the basement grow over trays of water. Aluminum reflectors and white-painted cement-block walls maximize light utilization from the four 40-watt fluorescent lamps. These bushes are just starting to bloom after their cool rest in late fall.

TIMERS

Control fixtures with timers to turn on lights each morning, then shut them off each night. By using an automatic timer, you can provide just the right number of hours in each 24-hour period with no bother at all. I use appliance timers made by the Intermatic Corporation. Each timer accepts up to 875 watts.

When your light garden will be subject to heavy use, with possible splashing of water, wet floors, or similar shock hazards, use a three-wire grounded timer and fixtures. The three-wire grounding is a worthwhile safety feature costing only a dollar or two more.

LAMP TYPE

Beginning light gardeners are logically confused about which type of fluorescent lamp to use. While doing extensive tests for my *Complete Book of Houseplants Under Lights,* I discovered that miniature roses did remarkably well under modern broad-spectrum fluorescents.

This automatic timer has a three-wire plug and accepts a heavy electric load.

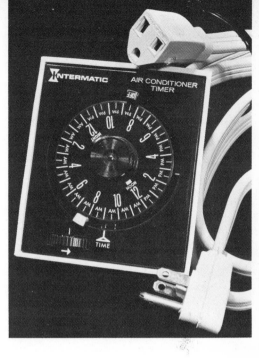

Several companies offer broad-spectrum lamps in popular sizes for light gardens (20 and 40 watts). Agro-Lite (Westinghouse) and Wide-Spectrum Gro-Lux (Sylvania) are specifically designed for plant growing. Vita-Lite, Naturescent (Duro-Lite Company), and Tru-Bloom (Verilux Company) are broad-spectrum lamps with daylight color blending perfectly with natural light. These lamps were not developed for horticulture, but they are useful in growing plants. When you give roses light from broad-spectrum fluorescents, it is not necessary to provide any incandescent light, even if fixtures have sockets for screw-in bulbs. For several winters I have had many roses under Agro-Lite lamps with excellent results. Combinations of Wide-Spectrum Gro-Lux and Vita-Lites also grow fine roses.

LIGHT HOURS

Roses grow and flower most rapidly with long 12 to 18-hour days. When saving electricity is important, or if you wish to have roses grow more slowly, provide 12 hours of light. For average winter flowering, with no special need to push plants, set timers to a 14-hour day.

To obtain maximum growth, which is useful with seedlings and important cuttings, or in order to meet show schedules or for hybridizing programs, give roses 16 to 18 hours of light per 24-hour period. If your plants receive some sunlight, set timers to supplement daylight during light hours,

The lights above these roses are timed to go on at sunrise, then remain on several hours after sunset. This small area serves as an isolation place for new roses; they are not placed with other indoor plants until I am sure they are bringing in no pests. Some sunlight comes in the window.

then burn into the night until total desired time is reached. Avoid giving roses 24 hours of continuous light.

DISTANCE

Adjust lamp-to-plant distance for compact growth unless you want long stems. Bushes farther away than 3 to 4 inches under tubes will grow and flower but take more room as stems reach for light. Set short plants and seed flats on inverted pots or blocks of styrofoam to get them close to the lamps. Keep a watch on bushes starting to bloom: buds actually touching the tubes may scorch.

LAMP LIFE

Count on a lamp life of 1 year for growing roses entirely dependent on fluorescents. After a year of use fluorescents lose much intensity. Often the ends start to darken, and plants may not grow as well. If roses get some sun, you might change lamps every 18 to 24 months, to save money.

'Willie Mae' grew especially well under lights when roots developed outside the pot in a tray of moist perlite. The pot had to be cut apart when the bush was transplanted.

When changing lamps, put in one new lamp, then wait a month before replacing another. This gives foliage a gentle transition from older dim lamp to bright new tube.

SELECTION OF ROSES

The best hybrids to grow under lights are the ones you like best, but keep an eye to how much room you have available. Usually light gardens are somewhat restricted, for reasons of available space and budget. If you can supply room and enough light, there are no restrictions on the miniatures to grow. In fact, you can even grow trailers in a basket, but most of us have less available space, so the compact to micro minis are best.

Check growers' catalogs for hybrids that remain less than 8 inches tall. Some hybridizers, such as Ernest Schwartz, are breeding micro minis especially suited to light gardens. Remember that even micro minis may

Recently potted roses have been trimmed back and will rest outdoors until early winter. They may be brought into the light garden in stages for a series of flowerings.

grow larger than listed when you give them rich soil, warmth, and good light. Fortunately, you can keep branches well under 12 inches by pruning as you cut flowers. The hybrids that require minimal pruning to stay small are listed as micro minis in chapter 3.

14
Greenhouses
and Sunrooms

You can control greenhouse and sunroom temperature to suit miniature roses perfectly. By varying temperatures, you can make roses stop growth and go into dormancy or grow at any speed from poke-along to inches per week.

Miniature roses will grow along with many intermediate to cool-growing greenhouse crops. I have even grown mini roses among tropical orchids, with 70 percent relative humidity and 68°F. nights. However, the ideal sunroom and greenhouse conditions are 60° to 65°F. nights with 50 percent relative humidity. Slightly warmer conditions will encourage new growth on propagations, while cooler nights will slow down growth.

COMPANIONS

Suitable greenhouse companions include chrysanthemums, cool to intermediate orchids, spring bulbs, Rieger begonias, temperate-region bonsai trees, potted lilies, and geraniums. These are practical in home collections. For commercial production it is more efficient to restrict roses to their own house.

LIGHT

In all regions where winters are cool, roses thrive under clear glass from October to February. In sunrooms you will never have to provide shade unless the roof is glass. In a greenhouse, slight shading on the glass may be required when spring sun begins to get hot, usually late February or

Inexpensive plastic coverings are suitable for greenhouses where winter temperatures do not drop below freezing for long. However, plastic tears easily. This house in California protects stock miniature roses growing in 1-gallon cans.

March. Fiberglass greenhouses and well-cooled houses where temperatures remain below 85°F. will do without shade.

Mini roses under glass will accept strong sun if humidity is high and temperatures not excessive. Foliage may burn when interior temperatures shoot up, humidity drops, and the sun is close. These conditions are likely to occur during summer months.

RAISED BENCHES

Potted roses prosper on raised benches of wood, wire, or cement. Spacing is important, since crowded bushes fail to make symmetrical growth. Most mature minis need a space 10 by 10 inches square. The micro minis need less, while the larger modern hybrids can occupy much more if not pruned tightly.

CONTAINERS

Miniature roses can, of course, be planted in ground-level greenhouse beds or in raised, well-drained benches, but they are easier to manage if confined to containers. Some well-designed sunrooms have raised beds built of stone or redwood. These are often filled with soil, and plants are set free. However, in sunrooms, even more so than in greenhouses, it is an advantage to keep roses in their own pots so bushes can be turned or replaced easily.

For large collections or commercial rose crops, keep all pots of a given size on the same bench. Within a given pot size, say 8-inch pots for mature bushes, group the specific hybrids together. Each clone has its own style of growth. You will find extensive collections easier to care for if identical plants are grouped. The exception to this system might be a bench designated as a display area for mature bushes of many cultivars, each in containers of maximum size for miniature roses, usually 1 gallon. These specimen bushes will also furnish cuttings at least once per year, pruned just before they are given a rest.

Delicate pink 'Dresden Doll' shines in a sea of dew-kissed foliage. In a humid greenhouse or sunroom, moisture condenses as temperatures drop, creating jewels of dew.

Basket-planted minis thrive hung from the greenhouse rafters or directly next to south or west windows in sunrooms. An efficient way to utilize space is to have pots of roses on benches or tables, baskets hung from above, and propagations under the benches with supplementary fluorescent light.

ROOTING PERIOD

In greenhouse culture and sunrooms where you can control overall temperatures, provide a cool humid rooting period for newly potted roses. Prune back to branched sections 6 to 8 inches above the soil for medium to large-growing hybrids. The micro minis usually need only a slight trim, removing an inch or two from the tips of branches to encourage root growth and new flowers.

Only prune roots if they are too large for the pot size you want to use. Most mini roses propagated from cuttings, and those received from commercial growers, will need no root pruning. Roses dug up from garden or greenhouse beds, but destined for containers, may need one-quarter to one-third of their roots pruned, in balance with the top growth removed. Be sure not to prune roots without also removing a similar portion of top growth.

WATERING

Watering roses in a greenhouse can be done automatically. Hybridizer Ralph Moore keeps his roses healthy under the hot California sun with sprinklers set in each greenhouse bench. Another popular system uses individual 1/8-inch weighted hoses dropped into each pot. This is a practical method for 6-inch or larger pots.

The individual mini hoses are plugged into a 3/4-inch diameter plastic hose pipe that runs along a rafter or is otherwise suspended at a level higher than the pots. When water is released into the large pipe, it trickles into each pot through the small hoses.

Professional growers often attach watering systems to a timer or solanoid control valve activated by a scale. On the scale is a plant of the same size as found throughout the greenhouse. When this master plant dries to a precise weight, the electronically controlled water valve is activated to water all plants attached to the mini-hose system. This efficient system is not too expensive but it is only practical with a uniform crop.

A thin plastic Chapin tube with a lead weight is part of an automatic watering system. The small-gauge tube connects to a larger feeder hose that leads to the main water supply.

FERTILIZER

A steady supply of fertilizer is needed by roses whenever they are making top growth. Only during December and January, when greenhouses and sunrooms are normally much dimmer and roses slow or stop growth, should supplemental fertilizer applications be suspended. If you are giving the roses bright fluorescent light, they will require constant feeding. Chapter 6 has general details about suitable fertilizers.

Soil Fertilizers

Roses in very rich soil require less fertilizer, but most growers prefer to use a peat-based mix and add fertilizer. The peat-lite mixes mentioned in chapter 12 are suitable for greenhouse plants. For growing more than a small quantity of roses, you will find it easier to mix slow-release fertilizer

To fully utilize heated indoor space, I like to pot several cuttings in each 4 to 6-inch container. This quickly produces a bushy display with several flowering branches.

directly into the potting mix. Use a product such as Mag Amp (7-40-6), which will provide nutrients for up to 1 year. The usual dose is 2 tablespoons per cubic foot of potting mix.

Roses potted in a mix with Mag Amp do not need additional fertilizer, but growth will be better if they also receive a water-soluble fertilizer every second week. This may be decreased to every fourth week when growth slows in the winter.

Water-Soluble Fertilizers

Fertilizers designed to be dissolved in water are easy to apply in a greenhouse or sunroom with a waterproof floor. Attach a fertilizer proportioner to the hose line, add a concentrated fertilizer solution to the device, and every time you water, a small quantity of fertilizer is supplied to the roses.

Mix fertilizer according to directions to provide a ¼ to ½-strength solution. Fertilize for three consecutive waterings. For the fourth watering use clear water to clean away accumulations of fertilizer salts.

Excellent formulas for this sort of application include highly soluble Peters 18-18-18, Miracle Gro 15-30-15, or their rose formula 18-24-16. Combining a water-soluble fertilizer program with slow-release fertilizer in the potting mix encourages maximum growth and flowering. Remember that fertilizer helps roses grow but it is *not* a cure for poor cultural conditions such as poor light, low humidity, or inappropriate temperatures.

HEATING SYSTEMS

For maximum efficiency and rose health, heating pipes or warm-air distribution ducts should be slightly lower than the rose pots. The warm air will rise, thus keeping air in motion and helping to prevent fungus problems. Hot water is an excellent system for heating. The pipes, normally covered with thin fins to expose more warm surface to the air, distribute heat evenly. A fan going 24 hours per day is the best way to prevent pockets of still cold air.

An important advantage to greenhouse rose growing is that you can have seedlings sprouting at any time and use them in hybridizing if you wish. Here seedlings blooming for the first time are already being used as female (pod) parents in Harm Saville's rose project.

Nonvented open flame natural gas burners are inexpensive to install, and the CO_2 given off is beneficial to plants. However, unless these stoves are kept clean, with pilots and flame adjusted for maximum combustion, harmful ethlyene fumes will cause buds to blast. This is a major problem in tight plastic or fiberglass greenhouses, less of a hazard in glass-glazed structures or sunrooms, which tend to leak more air.

Fully vented heaters are safer for plants. Even if flames are not at top efficiency, the harmful fumes are released outside. Electric heat is expensive in most regions. Certainly in the Northeast it is both expensive and unreliable because of power shortages and winter storms. If electric power is more reliable in your region, it is practical to use it for greenhouse heaters. In my greenhouses the heat comes from natural gas, with supplemental hot air recycled from an adjacent basement. Electricity is used for supplemental lighting but not for heat.

Warm Areas

In regions that are nearly frost-free, a greenhouse may require heat only a few weeks each year. Even then the heat is used only to keep night temperatures above freezing, since the sun raises daytime temperatures quickly. This is a situation when a portable electric heater with attached fan would be a practical heating method. If heat is required only a few nights each year, you may not wish to pay for a permanent heating installation of gas or oil.

COOLING SYSTEMS

During hot summer months greenhouse temperatures are difficult to keep below 90°F. without some sort of cooling system. Simply applying shade paint or slats is not adequate, since light must still be kept bright for sturdy growth. Roses will not die if temperatures remain high, but the flowers sometimes change color, blast, or stop developing until temperatures moderate.

The evaporative cooler is an efficient cooling device except in very humid climates. The system works on the principle of evaporating water as a cooling agent for hot dry air. The smaller units are practical for home greenhouses and for installation in an outer wall of sunrooms, glassed-in patios, and similar plant-growing areas. The actual size required to offer any given degree of cooling depends on the size (air volume) of the plant-growing area and the average outside humidity. Greenhouse firms listed in chapter 19 offer detailed advice applicable to your local conditions.

SUPPLEMENTAL LIGHTING

Roses produce most flowers when days are long. Short winter days will not stop miniatures, but bushes given 14 to 18-hour days, with supplemental fluorescent lighting, produce three or four times more flowers. If electric bills are too high or energy continues to be a problem, compromise with 14-hour days.

For seedlings or for show plants needed to produce at their maximum capacity, 18-hour days will give spectacular results. Fixtures to hang above greenhouse benches or sunroom display beds should have only narrow reflectors. The narrow reflectors allow most of the natural light to reach the roses. Even more efficient are strip lights with fluorescent lamps that have internal reflectors.

Sylvania, for example, offers Gro-Lux (wide spectrum) bench lighting in an 8-foot outrigger fixture that holds 75-watt, 96-inch self-reflecting lamps. The lamps have a built-in reflector, so no other reflecting surface is required to direct light downward.

Even without supplemental light this display of mini roses produces winter flowers in a sunny west window at Margaret Pinney's home.

If you are interested in adding light but want maximum fixture portability, hang 40-watt strip lights 8 to 10 inches above the roses from September to March, as a day-length control, or all year around as a supplement to insufficient sun intensity, as might be the case with lean-to greenhouses. Chapter 13 gives details about lamp types.

RESTING GREENHOUSE ROSES

Miniature roses grown the year around in a greenhouse will remain top producers longer if they are given a short resting period each season. This dormant period can be initiated after the bushes have been flowering well for 8 to 10 months.

These miniature hybrids have recently been potted for indoor sunroom or greenhouse culture. They are rooting well in new containers but will be kept under cool conditions until vigorous top growth is desired. Bushes are given ample space, to discourage fungus attacks.

Reduce temperature so that nights fall to between 50° and 55°F. Prune back roses with care to keep the centers open by removing overly congested crossing branches. Remove any diseased or dead wood. How drastically you prune depends on your goal.

If you wish plants to remain as small as possible, then prune tops and roots together, in order to keep bushes from becoming drastically pot bound. However, I think it is more appropriate to grow mini roses in 6 to 8-inch pots or even gallon-sized containers. This permits abundant top growth with a corresponding increase in flower production. To produce cut flowers for showing or arrangements, you will want to have as many large branches as possible.

After bushes are pruned back and given 4 to 8 weeks of cool nights, they will slowly begin top growth. It is quite possible to stagger your crop if you wish. Some of the bushes can be kept in suspended growth by giving them 35° to 40°F. nights. Others can be started growing faster by providing standard 60° to 65°F. nights. To do this effectively, you will need a partitioned greenhouse or another house that can be kept cool. Otherwise, put bushes outside in cold weather to hold them (see chapter 9 for cool-rest methods).

The 65°F. night temperature results in the maximum number of flowers because growth is fairly rapid. In northern regions, where winters have many dull days, I prefer slightly lower temperatures at night (to 60°F.) to assure slow, steady growth. When spring arrives, light becomes more intense and days are longer, so night temperatures can go to 65°F. with no risk of spindly stems.

This original photogram shows some unusual foliage plants I grow in dim areas near indoor miniature roses. *Top left*, a creeping *Ficus pumila minima* and the slower-growing oakleaf form *quercifolia*. The large leaf at *bottom* is from trailing *Anthurium polyschistum*, a Colombian jungle vine; *top*, a sprig of delicate, white-flowered Tahitian bridal veil, *Gibasis geniculata*.

15
Indoor
Companions

Although miniature roses do bloom all year long, few of us want to grow *only* roses indoors. Fortunately, hundreds of lovely companion plants will also thrive under ideal rose conditions. Your indoor plant display can include both roses and numerous species from other plant families.

By growing suitable companion plants, your collection will always have some special spot of beauty. When your mini roses grow under fluorescents, there will be dim areas around the fixtures. These low-light locations are suitable for ferns, philodendrons, and compact ivy.

TOLERANCE

Mini roses are tolerant of many different combinations of humidity and temperature. They even grow with limited light, but I will assume that you want compact growth and average-or-better flowering on your roses. Therefore, companion plants should grow under the same conditions required for superior mini roses; 60° to 68°F. nights, bright light (sun or broad-spectrum fluorescents), a relative humidity of 50 to 60 percent, and good air circulation.

The companion plants are most desirable to provide foliage and flowers different from roses. By growing an attractive background of companion plants, you will insure that your roses show up better. The following are some interesting companions.

Some of the interesting tropical plants I found on this Costa Rican mountain slope are at home with indoor miniature roses because nights in this higher altitude fall into the 50's. Many plants from the tropics are useful rose companions for a light garden, greenhouse, or sunroom.

BEGONIAS

I love miniature begonias growing among mini roses. You may have to hunt for mini begonias, because they are seldom offered in supermarkets or chain-store garden centers. You can find the unusual types I mention in some of the mail order catalogs listed in chapter 19.

If you have specimen rosebushes in 6 inch or larger pots, you can grow mini *Begonia bowerae nigramarga* as a ground cover directly around the rose. Begonias to grow in their own pots, placed among rose containers or toward the edge in light gardens, include dwarf rex cultivars such as 'Wood Nymph', 'Shirt Sleeves', and 'Robin'. Any of the hybrids you see listed as *Begonia bowerae* offspring will have compact growth 1 to 3 inches tall, and lovely silver hairs along the leaf margins. These begonias grow well from leaf cuttings or stem tips rooted in water or vermiculite.

Flowers

For constant flowers, grow dwarf hybrids of the wax begonia *B. semperflorens*. It is fun to grow these from seed, but you can obtain

246

healthy plants at local garden centers in the spring. The new 'Carefree' strain includes some 6 to 8-inch tall bushy types in rose, red, and white.

Rieger Hybrids

Semituberous Rieger begonias have brilliant pink, yellow, orange, or red flowers on bushy plants with oval glossy leaves. Growth is upright on 'Schabenland' selections, arching to pendulous in 'Aphrodite' cultivars. All winter long my mini roses grow side-by-side with Rieger begonias. Both plants thrive where air circulation is vigorous, since the Riegers, like roses, are attacked by mildew.

Rieger hybrids grow from 1 to 2-inch woody tubers, but commercial propagation is done from stem cuttings, leaf cuttings, or tissue culture. Blooming specimens are usually offered by retail garden centers during Christmas to Easter holidays.

After blooming well for 4 to 6 months, Rieger begonias will look bedraggled. You can return them to perfection by making stem-tip cuttings or resting old tubers in their original pots for 4 to 6 weeks, then repotting in 6 to 8-inch pots. Soak soil once, then mist daily with warm water until growth begins. Water only on soil when leaves appear.

Larger begonias, such as the floriferous Angel Wing types, do well with mini rose conditions. They are practical in spacious windows, greenhouses, or sunrooms. Smaller hybrids are best in light gardens and are in better scale with miniature roses. 'Tom Ment' is one fine compact Angel Wing with silver-spotted foliage and orange flowers.

BULBS

The small spring-flowering bulbs, such as crocus and miniature narcissus, mentioned in chapter 8, are suitable, though short-lived, indoor companions. To have a good show with spring bulbs, you must give the planted bulbs a 10 to 12-week cool, dark rooting period. Garden shops that offer these bulbs each fall usually have free folders that show in detail how to plant and force bulbs.

Less bother, and lasting for years with indoor culture, are several of the tropical bulbs. The 8 to 10-inch tall *Cyrtanthus* from South Africa will bloom in a few months from seed. I grow the new hybrids from Thompson and Morgan Seed Company. These have pastel-colored, tubular-shaped yellow, pink, and rose flowers from small underground bulbs. Foliage is narrow, glossy, almost grassy. The group I grew next to roses in the basement produced flowers in 5 months from seed.

Dwarf amaryllis thrive alongside roses, but the 4 to 6-inch flowers are out of scale. Similar in shape but growing only 6-inches tall are the rain lilies *(Habranthus)*. Foliage resembles that of *Cyrtanthus*, but flowers appear as single blooms twice each year with good culture. They look like tiny amaryllis and many are fragrant.

Leaves on the Amazon lily *(Eucharis grandiflora)* look like the shiny dark green foliage of Aspidistra. Flowers appear on 6 to 10-inch stalks opening greenish-white and maturing to stark white. The eucharises I collected in the Peruvian Amazon basin grew in mud, but were subjected to wet and dry periods alternately every few months, depending on the season.

In captivity the Amazon lily thrives in a 3 to 4-inch pot with bulbs just under the soil or with tops slightly exposed. Maximum flowering occurs when bulbs fill containers with roots. Eucharises require less intense light than do roses, so they are useful at the ends or edges of light gardens and on windowsills shaded by the roses.

Pot crocus bulbs close together for indoor growing. This provides a good show in limited space. In spring, after flowers fade, plant hardy bulbs in the garden.

Cyrtanthus Thompson and Morgan hybrid

SUCCULENTS

Compact cactus and other moderately sized succulents require bright light, but much less water than do roses. Succulents are easy to care for and furnish interesting variations in an otherwise uniform sea of rose leaves.

Trailing and creeping sedums and crassulas can fill in under upright roses, on a windowsill, or on a light-garden shelf. Succulents with silver, gray, or patterned leaves are a beautiful contrast to rose foliage. Some suitable dwarf succulents are found in the genera *Crassula, Echeveria, Kalanchoe, Pachyphytum,* and *Stapelia.* Dwarf aloes and haworthias

These 'White Christmas' and 'Christmas Cheer' jungle cacti need a cool fall rest with long nights, so they stay outdoors with my roses until just before frost.

need less intense light than cacti but are just as interesting, require little care, and mature at 1 to 4 inches. Check specialists' catalogs for these unusual miniature succulents. Abbey Gardens in California offers an outstanding assortment.

ORCHIDS

I doubt if orchids ever grow alongside roses in the wild, but indoors many genera will bloom right next to mini roses. The larger, showy cattleya-type orchids tend to have coarse foliage and pseudobulbs. But I have found several small-growing orchids that are in better proportion with miniature roses. A few dwarf hybrids of *Cattleya* are also suitable.

Compact paphiopedilums (lady-slippers), miniature oncidiums, epidendrums, hybrids of *Sophronitis,* all are small enough to look nice with a

Deep orange *Potinara* Cherub is another 6 to 8-inch tall cattleya hybrid that will grow well with mini roses. Parents are the dwarf *Cattleya aurantiaca* X *Lowara* Trinket.

A compact, 6-inch tall hybrid of *Sophrolaeliocattleya* California Apricot X *Slc.* Jewel Box grew perfectly under broad-spectrum fluorescents, right next to miniature roses.

Glowing orange *Sophrolaelia* Psyche thrives under broad-spectrum fluorescents in my basement. Flowers last a month in perfection.

Paphiopedium Nisqually *(P. sukakulii* X *P. appletonianum)* is one of many compact tropical lady-slippers that thrive indoors under lights. Foliage on this hybrid is motled with silver green; flowers are tan and green and have brown hairs.

miniature rose collection. *Phalaenopsis luddemanniana,* a moth orchid with fragrant waxy red and white flowers, accepts cooler nights than most species in this genus and thus is an ideal rose companion. Hybrids of *P. luddemanniana* and other miniature moth orchids do well under fluorescent lights, and many are fragrant. New unusual hybrids are offered by specialists such as Freed, and Jones and Scully, listed in chapter 19.

GESNERIADS

Most of the African-violet relatives accept 60° to 65°F. nights and thus grow well with mini roses. Those gesneriads most appropriate in size and cultural requirements include: African-violets (*Saintpaulia* hybrids), especially the new strain of everblooming Ballet hybrids, named after women and bred by hybridizer Arnold Fischer. These were developed to make quick growth, adapt to varying conditions easily, and constantly produce large clusters of blooms. Some of my favorites are 'Lisa', a frilled

Saintpaulia 'Pixie Blue'
in a 3-inch plastic pot

pink; 'Ulli', a dark blue; and 'Dolly', a white double with petals edged blue. Since the African-violets grow low and in a spreading rosette, they tuck nicely under taller mini roses.

Another group of African-violets suited to miniature rose collections are the miniature trailers such as 'Pink Trail' and 'Pixie Blue' bred by Lyndon Lyon. When grown at a sunny window or under the roses, with broad-spectrum fluorescent lamps, these modern *Saintpaulia* hybrids are outstanding.

Columneas are mainly trailing plants, although a few rare species grow stiffly upright. My favorites are new everblooming hybrids. If pinched frequently, even the trailers form bushy pot plants. *Columnea* 'Mary Ann', a red hybrid with succulent shiny foliage, has been in bloom for three years under Wide-Spectrum Gro-Lux lamps; *C.* 'Red Spur' is another vigorous trailer with large true-red flowers.

Avoid growing the colored-leaf episcias with mini roses unless you keep nights above 65°F. At cooler temperatures the episcias look almost dead. One hybrid with white-fringed flowers, 'Cygnet', will accept cool nights but the foliage is plain green.

Gloxinias (*Sinningia* hybrids) are suitable in the new dwarf strains bred by Ted Bona and other hybridizers. These grow from underground tubers and after producing a cluster of red, red and white, pink, or pure white flowers, they will go dormant in a month or two. Rest them right in their pots until growth resumes. Even smaller are miniature *Sinningia* hybrids, but these are best in terrariums.

Kohleria hybrids grow from underground scaly rhizomes, forming upright 8 to 20-inch stems of fuzzy foliage, then clusters of flowers resembling foxgloves, in shades of pink, rose, or red, often spotted white or dark red. Species I found growing in Central and South America had rhizomes creeping in humus over well-drained ground, the tops of stems in bright light, with roots shaded with low shrubs and grass. *Kohlerias* will go dormant after flowering and can be stored in their pots until sprouts show. Compact hybrids include *K.* 'Princess' (dark pink) and 'Connecticut Belle' (pink with red markings).

Streptocarpus is a genus of fibrous-rooted African gesneriads with trumpet-shaped flowers in white, purple, blue, and pink. Most suited for rose companions are the newer Nymph hybrids, such as 'Constant Nymph' (blue) 'Ultra Nymph' (dark purple blue with black lines), and 'Maassen's White' (pure white). These thrive in unmilled sphagnum moss or one of the peat-lite mixes and tolerate cool nights. Prune leaves back ⅓ from tips if they get so long that they do not fit your space.

GERANIUMS (*PELARGONIUM* HYBRIDS)

Dwarf geraniums are durable, slow-growing plants that thrive under mini rose conditions. A series of true miniatures, 3 to 6 inches tall yet flowering size, are offered by specialists Merry Gardens and Logee's. Adaptable yet still miniature when blooming are dark red 'Bumblebee' and starry white 'Artic Star'. Both grow well next to my mini roses under lights.

Growing slightly faster and taller are new strains of modern geraniums offered as seed. Where space, light, and air are abundant, these are a fine choice. Flowers are now equal in quality to named vegetative geraniums. You can order seed for a mixture of colors or color-sorted types in white, pink, and scarlet. Seed-grown plants in the Sprinter series will bloom in 16 to 18 weeks.

Pelargonium (geranium) 'Bumblebee'

This *Pelargonium* (Martha Washington-type geranium) 'Springtime' grew in my cellar with miniature roses. Flowers are white and pink.

'Sugar Baby' trailing geranium

TRAILERS

Trailing ivy geraniums thrive in moist, cool locations but also need strong light. This combination of factors is difficult to provide, but some newer trailing hybrids are somewhat tolerant of less than ideal conditions. The dwarf pink 'Sugar Baby' is one nice selection that will do well with roses.

FOLIAGE

In the geraniums are some hybrids with colored foliage, such as 'Mrs. Burdett Coutts' (pink, cream, white leaves) and 'Jubilee' (golden green, brown leaf ring, salmon flowers). Other geraniums, sometimes listed as *Pelargonium* cultivars, are appreciated for fragrant foliage. The fragrant-foliage geraniums are easy to grow and will do well indoors or outside in window boxes. Strawberry or 'Countess of Scarborough', is a compact glossy-leaved selection of *P. scarborovide* with a most unusual refreshing perfume. The small gray leaves of open-growing *P. fragrans* 'Nutmeg' smell like a chest-rub cold remedy. 'Prince Rupert Variegated' is a small crinkled white-edged leaf on a compact bushy plant, scented of lemon.

This shallow dish garden grows at the side of one light fixture over my basement rose garden. I planted this tiny landscape with moss; *center*, fern sporlings *(Polystichum tsus-simense); left*, *Pteris* species; *lower right, Cryptanthus fosterianus.* A section of coral rock creates a dramatic mini mountain.

16
Propagation

One reason miniature roses are so popular is their willingness to propagate quickly without complicated or expensive methods. Gardeners all around the world are learning how to make cuttings from miniature roses, since most modern hybrids root quickly from branches, indoors or out. One bush can supply enough cuttings for 15 or 20 plants in a single season.

Growing miniatures from seed is another exciting way to get more plants. Even more fun is growing different types of roses from seed you produce yourself. With some degree of concentration and a few years of work, several amateur growers have produced hybrids of such merit that their mini rose creations are now offered by commercial rose growers.

For example, the floriferous, lightly perfumed mini 'Seabreeze' was grown by amateur hybridizer Marilyn Lemrow from Long Island, New York, then introduced by Nor' East Miniature Roses. Hundreds of backyard gardeners are now growing their own hybrids, not for commercial release, but for the constant excitement of seeing what will result from their own hybridizing efforts.

At my own garden in southern New York I find growing roses from seed an enjoyable way to learn about plant genetics. By careful selection I obtain seedlings that are well adapted to our conditions and my specific taste. Hybridizing for a specific goal, for example to create a moss-covered mini, as done by Ralph Moore, usually takes many years; but growing miniatures from seed, just for your own pleasure, requires only a single growing season. I regularly bloom roses from seed in three months, even in the winter when I grow them under fluorescent lights.

These miniature rose stem cuttings will soon be new bushes. Recently matured branches root easily for asexual propagation, producing roses just like the donor plant.

Hybrid tea roses, such as this one held by hybridizer Ralph Moore, are frequently used in breeding miniatures because they form, *right*, large hips with abundant seed.

SELECTING PARENTS

Miniature rose hybrids produced in recent times are crosses with larger-growing hybrid teas, floribundas, and climbers or shrub roses. Fortunately for the miniature rose breeder, seedlings from a miniature father (pollen parent) and large-growing mother (seed or pod parent) generally turn out to be miniature growers. Most of the commercial crosses are now made by placing miniature rose pollen onto flowers of larger roses. This gives a better seed set, more seeds per hip, and increased viability.

Which roses to use as parents depends on the final goal. If you only want to experience the thrill of growing roses from seed, it is enough to plant seed from any hip that forms on a miniature rose. The so-called species *R. chinensis minima* clones often set seed without being especially pollinated, although the bees do help. Another way to obtain a relatively good seed set is to mix pollen from several of your favorite roses, including some larger roses. Use this mixed pollen to set fruit on miniature parents such as 'Yellow Magic', 'Anytime', 'Darling Flame', or *R. chinensis minima.*

A somewhat more scientific method that I prefer is to select parents on the basis of desirable characteristics, then try to combine favorite traits from each parent in the resulting offspring. For example, if you like 'Gold Coin'

Henri Mandoux, hybridizer at Meilland Roses in France, showed me these two examples of miniature roses to illustrate female fertility. The hybrid *at the left* forms fruit easily and thus in an average garden it will produce fewer flowers once hips begin to form. *At right* is the type of female-sterile mini hybrid that is better for the average garden because it sets no seed to slow flower production.

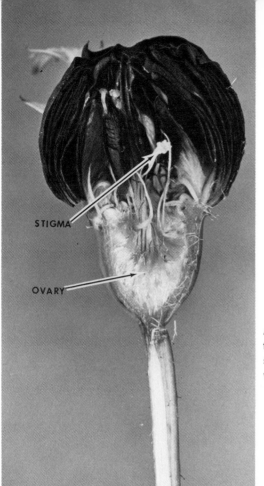

STIGMA

OVARY

A sliced-open bud shows that the stigma is attached to a long style, which leads to the ovary, where seed develops.

but would prefer somewhat more substance and perhaps color variations of orange to apricot, you might cross 'Gold Coin' with a heavy-substanced orange to red floribunda like 'Castenet'. For personal help with rose hybridizing, join the Rose Hybridizer's Association as outlined in chapter 18.

SEED

Each rose grown from seed will be different. Even with the so-called species seed sold as *R. chinensis minima* you will see a wide variation in the seedlings from singles to full pompom doubles, ranging from white to dark pink. With controlled crosses between two different roses you will see an even greater range of variation in offspring.

New hybrids are created by crossing select parents, sowing seed, and

Sexual reproduction from seed produces plants that differ from parents—a slight differentiation with self-pollinated species, a great one with hybrid crosses. For pollination to occur, ripe pollen germinates on the sticky stigma and pushes a long pollen tube down the style into the ovary, where sperms are released to unite with eggs, thus causing seed to develop.

finally selecting the best offspring for vegetative (asexual) propagation. With miniature roses the selected seedlings are propagated by cuttings rather than buds grafted onto a different rootstock. In contrast, the larger-growing hybrid teas, climbers, and floribundas are universally sold as bud-grafted plants, the rootstock being different from the rose on top.

POLLINATION

Open pollination occurs with roses grown outdoors, where bees can pollinate the flowers. If you wish to make a controlled cross, you must first remove the anthers containing pollen from the pod (female) parent before the pollen is ripe. Select a bud just showing color on the rose you wish to use as the female parent. Gently pull off all the petals and cut away the pollen-bearing anthers.

Once the anthers are gone, bees tend to ignore the flower. However, to be sure no unwanted pollen creates seed, I cover the emasculated pod parent with a dome of aluminum foil or small plastic bag. Commercial hybridizers frequently use weatherproof paper bags on which they write

The first step in controlled hybridizing is to remove petals on the female parent.

With all petals removed, the hybridizer can reach stamens, which he will remove to prevent a rose from self-pollinating. The unripe anthers on this rose will be cut off before pollen from the male parent is applied. Green sepals around the flower base form a collar called the calyx.

SEPAL

A female parent is being covered with a paper bag to prevent pollination by bees and pollen loss.

parent names or code numbers for each cross. The bags also guard seed that might be lost if the hip ripens and drops before being harvested. Other hybridizers do not bother to cover the seed parent, but they risk having bees complicate the work.

In two to three days the stigma or female organ should ripen and be receptive to pollen. Once the stigma is ripe, it will be slightly sticky, sometimes appearing wet. However, with some flowers it is difficult to judge the precise point of receptivity. To assure that the pollen will cause seed to form, I put the pollen on the stigma right away, then cover the flower.

Pollen is thus protected from being washed away or stolen by insects. As soon as the stigma is sticky, the pollen will sprout and push a pollen tube into the ovary, where male cells will be released and the cross consummated. Seed then forms.

POLLEN COLLECTING

To have the pollen you want ready at all times, collect just-opening buds of the male parent. Snip out the anthers and set them on a paper to dry. Small cardboard boxes as used for jewelry, glassine envelopes, or small glass jars are useful for storing dry pollen. Ralph Moore keeps different pollen in carefully labeled baby food jars. The important thing is to avoid wetting the pollen or keeping it in a humid place where mold may develop.

Miniature rose anthers are dried for at least several hours to collect pollen for hybridizing.

If you wish to save pollen for several weeks, store it with a small bag of silica gel to dry out the air around the pollen. Several bottles of pollen set in a plastic bag or sweater box with silica gel will keep well. Some commercial hybridiziers use a desiccator to dry pollen, but dry air or sun will do just as well.

PLACING POLLEN

Dust pollen on the stigma with a moist fingertip or delicate brush. I prefer the fingertip method or disposable cotton swab applicator because it assures that pollen will not be mixed accidentally. If the pollen is viable and the female parent fertile, seedpods (called hips) will begin to form.

The standard roses produce more seeds per fruit and have a higher rate of germination for the seeds ripened. However, I have planted seed from miniature roses, and for noncommercial hybridizing the germination is quite sufficient. Some miniatures that form seed easily include 'Golden Angel', 'Anytime', 'Woman's Own', 'Gold Coin', 'Magic Wand', and 'Yellow Jewel'.

Once a hip begins to form, be sure to maintain good watering and fertilizing for the mother plant. In 4 to 6 months the hip will turn orange and feel slightly soft. This means the fruit is ripe and can be picked. Crosses made in June are generally ripe in October or November. Open the fruit,

Harm Saville hybridizes roses by transferring pollen with a slightly moist finger.

Above, Ralph Moore stores ripe pollen in baby food jars. He uses a small brush to apply pollen on female parent.

Right, Ernest Williams covers his pod parents with bags on which are written hybridizer's codes. Bags also protect any seed that may drop from prematurely ripening hips.

Top, hip of 'Golden Angel'; *bottom*, moss mini 'Paintbrush'

This hip on 'Toy Clown' is starting to turn orange, which indicates ripening.

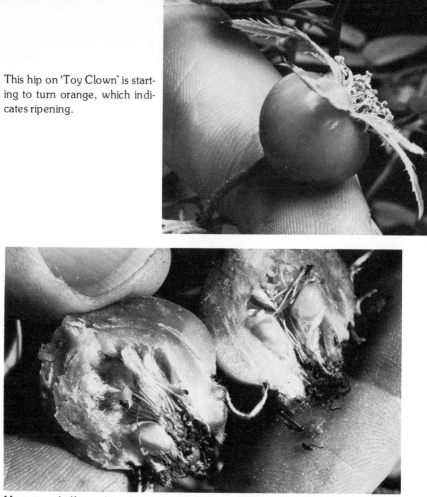

Here is a half-ripe hip showing only a few seeds inside. Many female-fertile miniatures develop only 3 to 6 seeds per fruit.

Here is fully ripe hip of shrub rose 'Sparrieshoop', showing numerous fertile seeds within.

pull each seed from the flesh, and dry the seeds in the sun or on paper toweling indoors for a day.

Dust the seed with Rootone-F (fungicide plus root-stimulating hormones). The seed must be chilled for 4 to 6 weeks before uniform germination can result. I plant the seed directly into a mix of Terra-Lite seed planting soil or a mixture of equal parts milled sphagnum, perlite, and vermiculite.

After planting, I water the seed flat, put it in a plastic bag, and set the whole flat in a refrigerator at slightly less than freezing for about 4 weeks, not more than 6 weeks.

The chilling period will cause most seed to germinate when the flat is later placed in a warm location. Growing seedlings under fluorescent light, with a 65°F. minimum night temperature, is the most efficient way. Seedlings will bloom within 3 months' time, but you will want to wait for the second flowering to fairly evaluate the new plants. Seedlings that you especially enjoy should be tagged and potted for further evaluation.

SPECIAL CONSIDERATIONS

Not all miniatures are fertile. Some that do have viable pollen or the ability to set seed do not exhibit this fertility all the time. Pollen on

Seed will be lightly dusted with a root-stimulating and fungicide powder, then planted in mixture of vermiculite, perlite, and milled sphagnum moss.

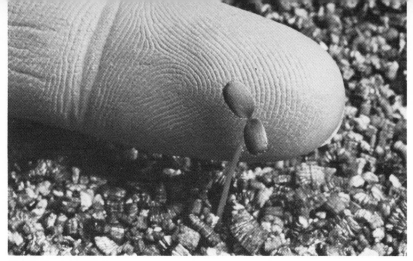

The first seed sprouts.

miniature hybrids tends to be quite meager, so several flowers may have to be harvested to collect enough for crossing onto larger roses. Finally, although many seeds may be formed, not all of them can be expected to germinate. Professional hybridizer Ralph Moore told me that he gets anywhere from 0 to 80 percent germination.

In general, larger roses used as seed parents produce more viable seeds than when miniatures are used as the pod parent. An important considera- tion in a long-range hybridizing program is identification of specific parents that are fertile and transmit desirable characteristics. Researching the background of miniature roses is informative. 'Peachy White', a recent in- troduction from Ralph Moore, has a background like this:

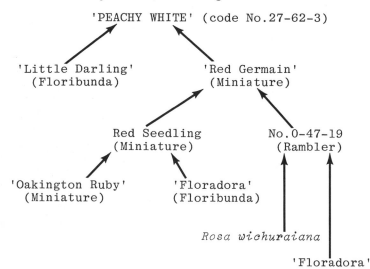

CUTTINGS

Propagation from cuttings is quick and relatively easy. Choose sturdy stems that have just finished flowering. Cut off the old flower stalk back to the point where you find the first complete leaf. Make stem cuttings 3 to 8 inches long. Short cuttings may root faster, but taller stems will grow just as well. Cut bottom ends just below a bud or bud with branch. Remove the leaf just above the bottom cut but leave on all other foliage.

Dust the bottom inch of each cutting with Rootone-F powder or a similar product. Tap off excess powder, make a 1 to 2-inch deep hole in a moist propagation mix, insert cutting, and firmly press around the base.

To root only a few stems, use a 3 to 4-inch pot. For propagating more stems, a small drained flat is most practical.

Once stems are in the mix, cover the whole container with clear plastic. To keep plastic from sticking to the foliage, use 3 or 4 small bamboo stakes, slightly taller than the stems, to hold the plastic above. You can usually put a whole pot or small flat directly inside a large plastic food bag.

Branch tips pruned from miniature roses are useful propagating material. These cuttings will be rooted in small plastic pots kept inside a plastic bag for several weeks.

Stems are trimmed for rooting, then dusted lightly with Rootone-F. Stems should be cut just below a live dormant bud, then the lowest leaf removed. *Left,* section has been cut from stem to be rooted; *right,* section has been dusted with powder.

Cover miniature rose cuttings with a plastic bag held away from foliage by small sticks or a bent wire.

274

This large outdoor rooting frame was built by miniature specialist and A.R.S. judge John Ewing. Plastic-covered top keeps in humidity and lets cuttings receive bright light for quick rooting.

Tie the open end to hold in humidity. Even with high humidity many leaves will drop from the cuttings, but rooting still continues. To keep mold from forming, remove the fallen leaves every few days.

Place the cuttings in a bright location but not in direct sunlight. Roots will also form well on cuttings kept under broad-spectrum fluorescent lamps. In about 3 weeks all stems should have begun to callus, then form roots. After 6 weeks roots generally will be seen growing out the bottom of each flat. By this time they can be transplanted into individual pots, to the garden, or several together into larger pots for a bushy indoor plant.

These cuttings I rooted under lights in the basement started to send roots out pot drainage holes a month after being set in rooting mix.

AFTER ROOTING

Water transplanted cuttings with the transplanting solution described in chapter 12. Shade the newly potted or garden-planted cuttings for several days, until their new feeder roots are established. I use leafy branches pruned off trees or shrubs to shade just-planted minis in the garden. Cheesecloth or very coarse burlap or even hay will also do the job. The idea is to reduce water loss from foliage pores until the roses can take up adequate moisture through new roots. Cuttings will begin to bloom about 3 months after being set down for rooting.

PROPAGATION UNDER MIST

Cuttings root quickly under a fine water mist. The commercial nurseries use mist systems controlled by automatic timers that fog the cuttings intermittently all day long. Stems rooted under mist accept much brighter light than stems only protected by plastic or glass. Ralph Moore at Sequoia Nursery roots thousands of mini roses in individual pots directly under the hot California sun by using a mist system. This way the cuttings do not lose water from the foliage and stems are kept cool by the water and thus can accept strong sun, which helps them grow quickly.

You can build an inexpensive nonautomatic mist propagation system with a garden hose and a mist nozzle. Select a nozzle, such as the Fogg-It, which puts out a very fine mist. Fasten the hose and mist nozzle to a post or hose clamp above the area selected for propagation work. Turn on the water just enough to get a fine mist from the nozzle. Very little pressure will be required.

Place flats or pots with cuttings where the mist will surround them. Every morning turn on the hose; every afternoon, about one hour before dark, turn off the hose. Naturally, no mist will be required on rainy or very

Thousands of cuttings rooting under mist in California sun at Sequoia Nursery.

My miniature rose rooting-mixture experiments show that cuttings in perlite develop the most extensive roots, quickly followed by those in vermiculite. Slightly behind were cuttings in commercial seed-starting mix, which held too much moisture for best root formation. Roses from all three rooting materials developed well when transplanted to regular potting mix or into the garden.

cloudy still days. This inexpensive system will help you root cuttings even in direct sunlight. Cuttings rooted under mist in direct light will not require the transitional shade when planted out, but the mist must be reduced gradually.

After 3 weeks of all-day fog, begin reducing the mist by turning on the water later each day and ending it sooner. By the 6th week cuttings should have strong enough roots to survive without top mist. Be sure the soil or rooting mix remains moist. Weak $1/3$ to $1/2$-strength water-soluble fertilizer will get the rooted stems off to a quick start. Apply this as folar or ground solution several days after mist has been turned off.

By rooting 1 to 3 stems in a $2^1/2$-inch pot you can avoid having to transplant newly rooted propagations. A useful system is to fill pots with a peatlite mix over $1/2$ inch of gravel. Once roots form, begin a regular feeding program with water-soluble fertilizer or add slow-release granules to each pot.

Cuttings rooting under mist at Nor' East Miniature Roses

LAYERING

Trailing or climbing roses will form roots on stems that are partially cut through and pressed onto moist soil. This permits a root system to form before the stem is cut from the parent plant. To encourage roots, cut the bottom of a stem halfway through, or scrape along an inch of stem, cutting slightly into the wood. Dust the cut with a hormone powder, cover with an inch of soil, vermiculite, or perlite, then place a small stone on top of the wound area. After 6 weeks enough roots should have formed to permit safe cutting from the main plant.

An alternative system, useful for propagations to be moved, is to layer stems in flats or pots placed next to the larger plant. Once roots have formed, you can cut the stem and move the newly rooted propagation easily.

Air layering is still another technique, used for the rare miniature that is reluctant to root with simpler methods. Prepare a stem for air layering by making an upward cut halfway through the stem at the point where you

279

wish roots to form—usually 8 to 10 inches below a mature stem is ideal. The stem may be branched above the cut.

Dust the wound with Rootone-F. Prepare a handful of wet, unmilled sphagnum moss to surround the cut. Squeeze the moss around the stem until it stays in place, then wrap clear plastic around the moss wad. Tie both ends with plastic-covered wire or twine to hold in moisture.

When roots form, you will see them just inside the clear plastic. Should the moss look dry before roots grow, add some water to keep it moist. Once a number of roots can be seen, cut the stem just below the root ball. You will have a rooted cutting ready to plant or pot, and the donor plant remains undisturbed.

LEGAL NOTES

Unlicensed vegetative (asexual) propagation of patented roses is illegal. Propagating patented plants for sale, even for nonprofit groups such as garden clubs, is a violation of the law. However, propagating personally owned plants for personal use on your own property is not going to bring a lawyer to your door.

Hybridizer Ralph Moore told me that he is happy home gardeners enjoy his creations enough to want more of them. He explained that so long as propagation is done for limited and wholly personal use, it is acceptable to him, even with his patented clones. Remember, though, that all hybrids still protected by patents should never be propagated vegetatively for profit or sale unless the propagator pays legally established royalties.

Patents protect new hybrids for 17 years, thus assuring hybridizers a fair chance to at least break even on their long-term plant breeding work. Hybridizers receive a few cents for each one of their patented roses sold under the usual license agreement. Once a patent expires, anyone can propagate and sell the plant legally without payment of a royalty. This is similar to copyright agreements that protect writing and music for a precise number of years before the works enter the public domain.

International Registration Authority For Roses

American Rose Center
Box 30,000
Shreveport, Louisiana 71130
Rose Cultivar Registration Application

No. _____
Date _____
Received _____
Approved _____

Proposed Name _____
Has this rose been disseminated under another name anywhere in the world? _____
If so, give synonyms _____
_____

Patented or Trademarked _____ No. _____
Originator _____ Code name _____ Year _____
Introducer _____ Year _____
Seed parent _____
Pollen parent _____
Mutation of: _____
Classification _____
Bud form: _____
Bloom - Size: Depth _____ Diameter _____ Form _____
No. blooms in cluster _____ No. petals _____
Thorns, shape _____ Color: _____ No. per 10cm. stem _____
Location _____
Fragrance _____
Describe Color _____
_____
Color Chart used _____
ARS Color Class _____
Describe foliage _____
Habit of growth _____
Quantity and continuity of bloom _____
In what way is this rose different or better than existing cultivars _____
_____
_____

Applicant _____
Firm _____
Address _____
I am a member of the American Rose Society and herewith enclose $5.00 (non-members must remit $15.00)
Signed _____
Approved: American Rose Society Registration Committee
Chairman _____ _____
_____ _____
_____ _____
Publication: Place and Date _____

New hybrids should be officially registered before being distributed. This is the international form used for roses.

17
Problems and Pests

Miniature roses prosper with much less care than is required for larger roses, perhaps because minis are easier to mulch, water, and feed. In any event, when the occasional problem fungus or insect does occur, the small bushes can be quickly treated. If you decide to carry on a regular preventative spray program against black spot and mildew, as outlined in chapter 10, you may seldom see any foliage problems.

The insects most troublesome are aphids, which suck sap from new shoots and buds; red spider mites, which are actually spider relatives rather than insects; and thrips, which cause buds to blast or distort.

Somewhat less persistent and easier to control are various beetles, caterpillars, and similar chewing insects. Larger chewing insects, such as Japanese beetles, can often be kept under control by simply crushing every one you find. However, if the infestation is large or your garden extensive, it will be necessary to use natural predators or some type of spray for full control.

Insecticides and fungicides are constantly being tested and revised by the manufacturers. At the same time, government agencies change regulations regarding spray materials, and local conditions may make one chemical slightly more effective than another. The spray materials listed below are nationally available products proven for use on roses and currently in use.

A squirrel ate all but two seeds in this hip of a hybrid I made outdoors on 'Golden Angel'.

Indoors, a slug relative called bush snails may cause damage. Control with slug baits or sprays.

Aphids sucking sap

Here is a list of the pests most likely to attack miniature roses and ways to control them:

Pest	Damage	Control
APHIDS Small green to black soft-bodied insects clustering on new growth	Suck sap, weaken plant, deform flowers	All-purpose rose spray such as Isotox or Orthene; also, wash away with hose water
BEETLES Found on outside of plants as adults, as larvae inside canes	Eat flowers, foliage, and canes	All-purpose spray; crush those you see
CATERPILLARS and BUD-WORMS	Chew buds and foliage, roll up leaves	All-purpose spray
MIDGES Flies about ½₀ inch long	Larvae eat flowers and foliage, roll up leaves	Malathion or all-purpose spray
SPIDER MITES Almost-microscopic sucking pests; form fine webs	Suck sap, kill leaves, weaken bushes	All-purpose spray that has miticide, such as Isotox, that contains Kelthane, alternate with Malathion; wash undersides of leaves with water frequently
THRIPS Tiny tan to yellow insects seen under petals	Suck sap and prevent buds from opening fully	All-purpose spray
WHITEFLY Active flying insects; live on undersides of leaves	Suck sap	Spray with synthetic pyrethrum (Resmethrin)

'Good beetles—the ladybugs, which eat aphids and mealybugs

Japanese beetles ruin flowers. Soon a synthesized sex attractant may be available as a bait for traps or as a spray. This new development lures male beetles into traps by smelling like virgin females. When used as a spray, the sex attractant disrupts mating activity. Beetle grubs have developed resistance to milky-disease bacteria, formerly an effective control.

Young grasshoppers on 'Gold Coin' will chew holes in petals. Chewing pests are controlled by birds, a strong hose spray, systemic granules, or finally, an overhead insecticide spray.

'Nancy Hall' eaten by a caterpillar

Spider mites and webs on mini rose foliage

Whitefly adult and young on underside of a rose leaf

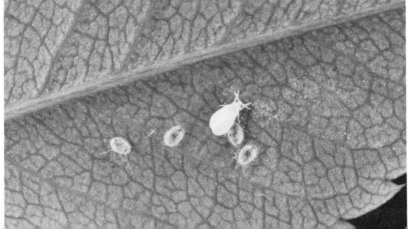

Chemicals that kill insects and related pests are available as dusts, systemic granules, smoke bombs, strips that give off fumes, and the traditional sprays to be mixed with water or used in the form of the more expensive aerosol products. A single insecticide may be available in several forms, so which to use depends on which is most effective against the pest and on which you find easiest to apply.

SYSTEMICS

The dry granules of systemic chemicals are applied to the soil, lightly scratched in, then watered thoroughly. The granules release an insecticide that is absorbed by the plant roots and is thus transmitted to all parts of the rose. When pests eat or suck the plant, they also receive a dose of the poison and soon perish.

Liquid spray-on systemics function in a similar way except that they are absorbed through leaf pores rather than through root hairs. In the case of all the systemics, the pests must *begin* to do damage before they are killed. This is in contrast to contact pesticides that kill any pest they touch. Some sprays, such as the all-purpose Isotox, combine systemic action with contact insecticides.

Dry granules of a systemic insecticide, combined with rose fertilizer 8-12-4, are a clean, simple way to control pests and fertilize roses.

287

Isotox contains a combination of pesticides that attack the common garden pests. The Isotox formula includes Meta-Systox R, Sevin, and Kelthane. Similar in action is a more recently introduced Ortho spray called Orthene.

I have used Orthene and Orthene combined with Phaltan fungicide on miniature roses and find it effective, although it has quite an unpleasant odor. The Orthene I tested is a powder formula, but Chevron Chemical Company reports that Orthene will be nationally available as a liquid concentrate. The recommended strength is 1½ tablespoons of Orthene in 1 gallon of water. Read the product label and attached pamphlet supplied with Orthene before mixing.

As a general insecticide Orthene kills aphids, thrips, mealybugs, whitefly, caterpillars, and even spider mites. The spray is biodegradable and has systemic action. The active ingredient in Orthene is Acephate (O,S-dimethyl acetylphosphoramidothioate).

Useful systemic granules for mini roses include Science Di-Syston granules (2 teaspoons per 6-inch pot) and the Ortho Systemic Rose and Flower Care, a fertilizer (8-12-4) combined with Di-Syston insecticide. These products protect roses for 4 to 6 weeks.

ALL-PURPOSE SPRAYS

Several companies offer sprays specifically formulated for roses. These often contain a miticide such as Kelthane to control the spider mites, plus several other chemicals designed to control a broad range of rose pests.

When these all-purpose sprays are combined with an effective fungicide, such as Benlate or Phaltan, they provide full protection to roses from fungus problems and insect pests. Remember that many of the larger insects may well be kept under control by birds, and even tiny aphids and spider mites can be swept away with a strong stream of hose water. Use restraint with insecticide applications until you see a real need for them.

DISEASES

Black spot and mildew are the most troublesome diseases for miniature roses. One way to minimize the occurrence of these diseases is to practice optimum culture, including full sun and good air circulation. Certain roses are more susceptible to black spot or mildew than others. For example,

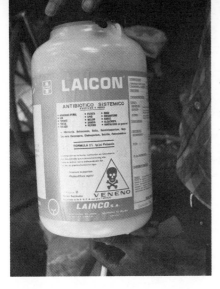

This dangerous-looking product is a systemic antibiotic used by Rosas Dot in Spain to control fungus on roses. All spray materials can be dangerous and must be used with caution.

'Crimson Gem' mildews before many other miniatures, even when sprayed with fungicides. So if mildew is a serious problem in your garden, avoid growing highly susceptible hybrids.

Black Spot

You will recognize black spot *(Diplocarpon rosae)* from the black spots on foliage, quickly followed by yellowing of tissue, then leaf drop. Black spot is harmful because unless controlled, the roses can lose so much foliage that they die. This fungus spreads by spores transferred in splashing water.

In regions with limited rainfall, black spot is seldom serious. But in most states it is necessary to spray with a fungicide every week from spring into fall to keep all black spot away. A mulch that stops rain from splattering lower foliage is an additional control. Remove all infected leaves and fallen foliage whenever practical, because these harbor the fungus spores.

Useful sprays for black-spot control (and for mildew too) are Phaltan (Folpet) and Benlate (Benomyl) fungicides. These two powders are used as sprays after being mixed with water.

Dilute Benlate at 1 tablespoon per 2 gallons of water. Add ¼ teaspoon of detergent or a commercial water-wetter (surfactant) so that the spray will stick to rose leaves. Apply every 10 to 14 days for prevention. If weather is wet, apply every 7 days. Use Benlate at 1 tablespoon per gallon if the weaker dilution is not effective.

Dilute Phaltan at 1 tablespoon per gallon of water and apply in 7 to 10-day intervals, or as necessary to control mildew and black spot.

POOR

NO FUNGUS

Black spot fungus has defoliated one miniature rose in this row of hybrid trials at Universal Roses in France. Resistant seedlings on either side have no fungus problems. Roses that show poor resistance are selected out; those that remain healthy, such as the bushes at top and foreground in this row, may be introduced to gardeners.

Wet powders with a slight quantity of warm water to make a paste (as when wetting flour for sauces); then dilute further for spraying. Benlate is absorbed into plant foliage; Phaltan adheres to leaves. You can mix these two fungicides at ½ tablespoon each per gallon of water. Add fertilizer to folar feed simultaneously.

I frequently use the Benlate-Phaltan-fertilizer combination to control mildew and black spot. Only when insects become a real problem do I add an insecticide to this same solution. Actually, studies have shown that Benlate and another fungicide, Karathane, partially control mites by upsetting their reproductive cycle.

'Wee Lass' holds onto foliage until fall because it is resistant to black spot.

'Kathy', planted right next to 'Wee Lass', has lost many leaves to black spot fungus because the plant is not as resistant. A chewing insect took some bites from one top-right leaf.

Powdery Mildew

Mildew most frequently occurs when the air is humid and still. Wet foliage is not necessary for mildew to begin, in contrast to the black spot fungus, although mildew is also caused by fungus. The mildew first attacks new leaves and flower buds, causing rolling of the edges, halting bud development, and eventually progressing to a white powdery material (mycelium) over the affected parts of each rose.

The white powdery mycelium is water resistant, and the actual fungus has parts inside the rose tissues, so any spray used to control mildew should be a fine mist applied to top and bottom leaf surfaces. It is also important to use a wetting agent unless fungicides are mixed with insecticides already formulated with a wetting agent. Since mildew increases by having spores blown about rather than by splashing water, it is important to spray *all* roses in the general area, not just those showing the problem.

High humidity and mild temperatures in the mid 60's to 70's are perfect conditions for mildew. By increasing air circulation indoors with ventilation and fans, you can often control mildew without regular spraying. Outdoors, spray if mildew starts, and continue during the growing season.

Apply a mist of Karathane, Phaltan, or Acti-dione PM (an antibiotic) according to package directions. With Karathane start at ½ teaspoon per gallon, since higher concentrations may damage foliage. Apply sprays when temperature is under 80°F.

Another effective material for controlling mildew is Benlate, described previously under black spot treatment. Rose specialists sometimes offer combination fungicides or fungicide-insecticide blends that usually contain at least one of the fungicides mentioned here.

Powdery mildew on 'Over
the Rainbow' foliage

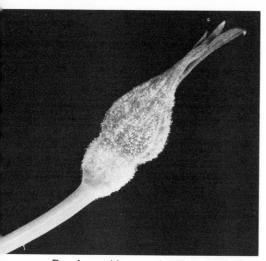

Powdery mildew attacks 'Sassy Lassy' bud

Root Rot

Fungus-causing root rot is seldom a problem in home gardens, but may appear in greenhouses or where roses are grown together in benches or flats—as for propagation from cuttings or seed. Truban fungicide is an effective treatment. Commercial nurseryman Lyndon Lyon reports using dry Truban sprinkled on roots and stems of troubled roses. I saw Truban being used on mini rose cuttings at Star Roses to prevent fungus problems on the benches filled with thousands of cuttings under mist. Fortunately, you will probably never experience rot problems in your roses if they are grown with good drainage.

Iron Chlorosis

A deficiency of available iron causes rose foliage to yellow and eventually fall, a condition called iron chlorosis. New foliage becomes so yellow green that veins appear much darker in contrast. The cure is to supply iron in the form of water-soluble powder. Sequestrene (Geigy Chemical Company) is highly soluble, forming a yellow green solution for application to roots or directly to foliage in spray form. Green Garde is a coarser

'Chipper' has developed a cluster of green leaflets in the center of a three-week old flower. This problem is rare but may be seen more often when roses are growing very fast in well-fertilized soil.

micronized form of iron (Encap Products Company), which is applied dry on the soil or in solution.

On potted roses it is convenient to sprinkle a teaspoonful of micronized iron around each stem before chlorosis appears, since iron is always needed for chlorophyll production.

18
Societies
and Shows

Join the American Rose Society to learn more about new roses as soon as they are introduced. Your membership includes the monthly color-illustrated *American Rose* magazine, which covers new roses and cultural requirements for all regions. For the yearly membership fee ($15.50) you also receive the *American Rose Annual* (a bound book); a copy of the helpful new *Handbook for Selecting Roses,* which contains color classifications and ratings; free use of a mail order library; invitations to local rose societies; an opportunity to participate in regional and national conventions; consultation service for rose problems; and a discount on books offered for sale to members.

The A.R.S. also sponsors attractive test gardens in many states and gives awards to the most outstanding roses. One pleasant way to join the A.R.S. is through a miniature rose specialist who offers free plants to anyone who becomes a new member of the American Rose Society. For example Nor' East Miniature Roses currently offers two free roses to new members.

If you are sincerely interested in hybridizing roses, join the Rose Hybridizer's Association to receive a quarterly newsletter with material furnished by rose hybridizers around the world. As a member of the Rose Hybridizer's Association, you also have a free consultation service from specialists. Current dues are $4.00 per year. Of special interest is the R.H.A. membership list, which helps you contact other growers with your same interest in creating new roses.

ROSE SHOWS

To exhibit miniature roses for prizes at rose shows, you must first contact the show officials, usually a show chairman, to obtain a printed schedule. The schedule outlines awards offered, the various divisions, and usually contains condensed explanations of judging procedures.

The shows now include special sections for exhibiting miniature roses, since this group of roses has increased more than any other type of rose grown. The sections for miniatures are usually divided into arrangements, single flowers, and sprays of several flowers on a single stem. Gradually the miniature roses are gaining attention equal to that long given standard-sized roses. The official judging of miniatures is still not as regimented or precise as that for large hybrid teas, because miniatures are newer on the show tables.

Over the past ten or twelve years the rapidly increasing popularity of miniatures has encouraged American Rose Society judges to develop fair judging standards that allow for inherent differences among miniature hybrids. Such a divided schedule, to judge floribunda types against other floribunda types, hybrid-tea-shaped flowers against similar cultivars, has

At the American Rose Society-headquarters test garden in Shreveport, La., I was able to study miniature hybrids under trial for A.R.S. awards of quality. You are invited to visit trial gardens for miniatures, now also established at Crosby Garden in Toledo, Ohio, and Rose Hills Memorial Park in Whittier, California. Some miniatures are also grown for display in many other public rose gardens around the country.

An arrangement of 'Mimi' (pink), 'White Gem', 'Scarlet Gem', and 'Crimson Gem' in an heirloom silver vase.

long been the practice for large roses. But during the early years of miniature rose showing the tiny flowers were often judged all together, against one another, regardless of their genetic backgrounds or floral form.

Articles and discussions have brought many A.R.S.-accredited judges to favor dividing minis into categories according to their flower size, growth habit, and flower form. Prize-winning American Rose Society judge Sylvia McCracken of the Spokane Rose Society (famous for miniatures) told me that many experienced judges evaluate miniatures according to types such as floribunda, hybrid tea, sometimes even an old-fashioned style, even if this is not a written rule in the show schedule.

Some exceptionally popular miniatures are given classes by themselves and do not compete against the general entry miniatures. For example, a recent show of the Spokane Rose Society judged 'Cinderella' and 'Starina' in separate classes, while all other miniatures were judged according to color classification and size.

The hybrids with flowers up to one-inch across were grouped as small minis, while others were listed as larger-flowered and judged against themselves. In this system a perfectly formed two-inch flower will not win over a similarly perfect three-quarter-inch flower just because it is larger.

STUDY THE SCHEDULE

If you are interested in showing your miniature roses, it is important to join the American Rose Society and your local chapter society as well. Obtain copies of past show schedules and the A.R.S. *Guidelines for Judging Roses*. At official shows the rules generally follow A.R.S. guidelines, although some local regulations may be different and judges are obliged to go by local rules if there is any question.

Most well-designed show schedules contain several pages of suggestions for the exhibitor. These are worth reading several times if you are about to enter your first show. As with all formal events in human society, a rose show is built on regulations. You may discover some rules that seem quite arbitrary or perhaps even objectionable. However, to enter the show you must follow the published rules or stand to lose points. Each rose show is slightly different. Although local rose societies tend to follow the American Rose Society national rules, each local group has the freedom to establish special classes and to formulate specific rules for its own show. Judges also differ in their experience and personal taste.

JUDGING

The A.R.S. follows other national plant societies in having an educational program for training new judges and for keeping accredited judges up to date on new hybrids. This plan works well, but personal preferences and legitimate individual interpretations of general rules remain. However, since each class is judged by several accredited judges, the rose shows offer everyone a fair opportunity to win ribbons in honor of horticultural achievements.

I have found American Rose Society judges and members-at-large to be an outstandingly friendly group. Almost invariably an experienced rose grower will delight in teaching a beginner how to find success with roses, including how to grow and show his or her favorite flowers. Be sure to visit with members of your local rose society before you start to show roses. The more experienced grower/shower can give you an abundance of hints directly related to your climate and the style of judging in your region. This experience is valuable if you wish to participate in the friendly competition of the rose shows.

BASIC SOCIETY JUDGING OF MINIATURES

The standard rules for showing miniatures, based on A.R.S. recommendations, are almost the same as general rules for all rose shows. These include the following:

Scale of Points for Judging Rose Flowers

Form	25 points
Color	20 points
Stem and Foliage	20 points
Substance	15 points
Size	10 points
Balance and Proportion	10 points
Total Perfection	= 100 points

This display of miniatures 'Starina' and 'Over the Rainbow' was made by A.R.S. judge John Ewing to demonstrate the English Box, a low water-filled container used to display cut flowers. The blooms are judged according to condition, color, and balance. No foliage is used.

Regarding the general interpretation of the points in each category, the local show schedule will carry an outline explanation of what the judges look for. In the show schedule for a recent official judging of the Houston Rose Society I found these definitions, adapted from the A.R.S. rules:

Form looks for a bloom at its most perfect phase of possible beauty . . . generally from one-half to three-quarters open . . . gracefully shaped with sufficient petals, symmetrically arranged in an attractive outline, tending toward a high center.

Color is made up of three factors: hue, chroma, and brightness. Hue gives visual impact to the eye and distinguishes one color from

I often display miniature flowers with unusual mementos, such as this black clay toad vase from Oaxaca, Mexico.

another. Chroma is the purity and intensity of the hue. Brightness is the clarity and vividness of the hue.

Substance indicates freshness . . . the quality and quantity of matter in the petals. It constitutes the texture, crispness, firmness, thickness and toughness of the petals and determines the degree of stability and durability of form and keeping quality of the rose.

Stem and *Foliage* looks for straight stems, of proper length to complement the bloom, with typical prickles or thorns, with the stem serving as support of the bloom and foliage. The foliage must be typical, undamaged, clean, well groomed, without spray residue or evidence of insect damage or disease and, in addition, sufficiently abundant and of proper size to complement the bloom.

Balance and *Proportion* of a rose specimen specifically relates to the overall pleasing appearance of the specimen. The concept of balance and proportion refers to the aesthetic view of the bloom in relation to the stem and to the foliage, as well as the stem in relation to the foliage and bloom, plus the foliage in relation to the bloom and stem.

Size refers to the actual dimensions of the bloom. The size should be typical of the variety for an allotment of 7 to 8 points (out of 10), rewarding a superior sized bloom with 10 points. All other things being equal, a good big rose will win over a good typically sized rose of the *same* variety. Size consideration is used to reward the exceptionally well-grown specimen.

When you plan to enter a local rose show, obtain the printed schedule. You should find a list of points and interpretations very similar to that shown above. If you understand these rules, your chance of winning prizes increases. Good luck!

PICKING ROSES

Pick roses when the bushes are well watered and reasonably cool. This means that early morning or just before dark are good times. Flowers picked in the full sun may begin to wilt slightly before you get them into a cool place. For the longest life in cut roses, pick buds just as they are opening at the top. Buds picked as color begins to show will open nicely.

Roses picked when they are already one-half to three-quarters open may fade in a day, depending on the hybrid. If you have more than a few blooms to collect, carry a water jar with you into the garden. Fill the jar or pail with warm fresh water (about 100°F.). Plunge the cut stems into the warm water quickly, right up to the flower base. After you have collected the flowers, put the water-filled container in the warmest section of the refrigerator, overnight or for several hours. After this stem-soak and brief cooling period, the blooms will last better in arrangements or for showing.

If you have picked the roses for a show, clean off the foliage with warm water and a soft cloth. Flowers and foliage should be as spotless as possible. Each stem should have at least one leaf, preferably a complete five or seven-leaflet leaf.

Roses shown at official A.R.S. events may not be altered with any

A water-filled Aqua Floral dome enlarges the beauty of pink 'Madelyn Lang'.

foreign substance. This means that foliage cannot be shined with oil, milk, foliage gloss, or other such materials.

Flowers must be pure, not groomed with egg white, clear glue, or any such materials designed to improve life or form. Some petals my be legally removed, but the less tampering you do with miniatures the better. The winning secret is in ideal culture to grow exceptional bushes with full perfectly formed, well-colored blooms that require a minimum of grooming.

SOLUTIONS

Some of the top judges and prize winners I spoke with use only plain clear water for cut roses. Others insist on using a preservative solution such as Floralife, or homemade mixtures of 7-Up or Sprite added to water. The

This bouquet of mini roses will last for many days in a water-filled old-fashioned cream jar.

kind of soft drink is unimportant, but the ingredients, sugar and carbonated water, slow down spoilage.

A cut-flower preservative, such as the popular Floralife, contains simple sugar to nourish foliage and a mild disinfectant, which keeps water pure by inhibiting bacteria. My tests with Floralife show little difference between flowers given the solution and flowers in plain clean water.

However, the reports of some rose growers about Floralife are so enthusiastic that I recommend you try your own experiment. Mix the preservative powder with fresh warm water according to package directions. The resulting solution is used just like water, and containers are not damaged by the Floralife in any way.

DISPLAY

Place cut roses away from bright sunlight. The sun will shorten cut-flower arrangement life by several days. If you have a favorite display that you wish to have last for the longest possible time, place the container in a refrigerator every night. Double-check that water levels remain high around the stems.

Precise position of miniature roses in an arrangement is difficult to achieve without using a soft, water-holding foam inside the container. I like the material called Oasis because it can be broken into small chunks and pushed into tiny containers. The rose stems are thus held firmly, and you can achieve the design you desire.

The spiked weighted devices called roses, familiar to flower arrangers, are somewhat less useful but are suitable for larger miniatures, especially in clear containers, where you might object to a filling of spongy green Oasis. Coarse clean sand or bird cage gravel (grit) are useful in smaller containers as an anchor for shifting stems. The bird cage gravel has another use for flower arranging; use a tablespoon of bird gravel in a detergent solution to

For this arrangement in a 2½-inch Wedgwood vase, I added sprays of airy white *Cerastium tomentosum,* a silver-gray-leafed creeping plant called snow-in-summer for its abundant flowers.

clean the inside of small clear bottles and vases. If you shake the washing solution and gravel, it will clean off inner areas you cannot reach with a bottle brush.

At Home

Combine mini roses with other plant materials for different arrangements. Even in the winter a few fronds from a houseplant fern will furnish attractive green among rose flowers. *Calluna* stems remain green outside even through cold winters, as do *Erica* branches, so both are year-long possibilities for miniature rose arrangements. A dried leaf or a few strands of interesting grass are also lovely with brightly colored miniature roses.

For Show

Arrangements made for show competition are judged according to a published schedule, as outlined for the plain cut blooms. A typical scale of

'Hi-Ho', a coral pink climbing miniature, looks charming in an arrangement with desert woods and stones.

points for arrangements would look like this actual example from a rose show schedule:

Proportion and Scale	35 points
Design	30 points
Condition	15 points
Color	10 points
Distinction	10 points
Total Arrangement Perfection	= 100 points

For an informal bouquet of miniatures I used a small copper pitcher to create an arrangement just 5 inches tall.

Study your show schedule to determine whether the arrangement must be miniature itself—under 6 inches tall or wide, for example—or if the only requirement is that miniature roses be predominant in the display. Both types of rules occur.

If you want to compete, start out by studying prize arrangements at local shows. Your own artistic talent and horticultural skill will usually determine how successful your displays are with the judges.

Get ready for rose shows by being sure that the names on your flowers are 100 percent correct. Useful aids for rose growers who show include, *right,* the book *Modern Roses,* which gives correct names of all registered hybrids and, *left,* the local show schedule booklet. *Lower left,* the small booklet is the *Handbook for Selecting Roses,* an annual publication of the A.R.S. that also lists correct color classes. Small pruning devices, extra labels, tags, vases, an air blower, and baster for filling vases complete the props. *Right,* rose is 'Stacey Sue', *background and left,* unnamed seedlings.

PROPS FOR PRIZES

In my television work, props are often a key element in the success or failure of a program, and so it goes when showing roses. Your props will consist of important things designed to help your miniature flowers appear at their best. Providing the most efficient props plus a few common but necessary tools such as pens and tags will increase your chances of receiving recognition for well-grown roses. Here are some important show props and the procedures they involve.

Before the Show

Labels with Names—In your garden or indoors under lights, your plants must be correctly labeled or you must have some means of confirming the registered name of each hybrid. Show entries are generally restricted to officially registered cultivars identified by their names, such as 'Cinderella' or 'Starina'. This information is found in the *Handbook for Selecting Roses* and in the book *Modern Roses*.

Keep bushes labeled in the garden if you plan to show roses. The *MP* on this tag means "medium pink," the official A.R.S. color classification for 'Trinket'.

To keep names straight on cut flowers, push water-filled tubes into Styrofoam block. Write names on block with ball-point pen by each tube. If you wish to re-use the foam block, apply masking tape along edge to receive the names and remove it when no longer required.

Several Plants of One Hybrid—If you are serious about winning a prize, it is wise to grow more than one bush of your favorite show hybrids. For example, if you know that 'Starina' has a good chance of getting a prize in your region, be sure to have several perfect flowers of this variety by growing two or more bushes. This protects your crop should one bush fail to produce a perfect bloom at show time.

Plastic Aquapic Tubes with Rubber Caps—To hold your mini roses use plastic tubes with rubber caps filled with lukewarm water or Floralife. The tubes called Aquapics have sharp-pointed ends. I push these into blocks of Styrofoam for a perfect stable holder of cut blooms. You may have to rub off thorns on the lower part of each stem to fit some roses through the rubber cap, or remove the cap and just use the tube filled with water.

Sharp Scissors—Prune roses with sharp clean scissors or mini shears (see suggestions in chapter 9). Cut flowers carefully, using tools that make a clean cut.

Waterproof Pen and Stick-On Labels—As you cut each bloom, it is important to label it correctly. In fact, it is a good idea to write out the name on a self-stick label *before* you cut the flower. Stick the label on the water-filled tube, then cut the bloom and put the stem in the labeled tube.

Cool Storage Area—Enthusiastic growers who show lots of roses devote a section of their refrigerator to prize flowers or even have an old "fridge" set to 35° to 40°F. They can thus hold miniature buds in cool suspension for several days. If you don't have a refrigerator, use a cool cellar or room. Keep flowers away from fruit.

Cool Carrier—When it is time to transport flowers to the show, put the blocks of styrofoam holding the Aquapics into a big insulated picnic cooler chest. If you have a long dry drive ahead, set some frozen picnic "ice" cans into the plastic cooler, but not touching the blooms. Protect flowers with a cone of thin tissue wider and open at the top, wrapped around the tube. This system works for growers from California, Florida, Colorado, New York . . . in fact anywhere. The secret is to pick tight buds, condition them well with warm water and cooling, then give them cool, moist transportation. If your trip from home is less than an hour and the season is not hot, you can do without the insulated cooler. Some of the prize-winning growers told me they ". . . just stick the flowers in an old Coke bottle and bring them to the show." For miniature roses I like the Aquapics better. Whatever system you use, the end result is to get your tiny roses to the show table in perfect condition. Once at the show, be sure to keep flowers out from under hot lights until the last possible moment. Some of the display boxes for cut flowers are illuminated with very warm incandescent reflector floods or spots.

At the Show

Full Show Schedule and Rules—This is something you read before coming to the show, then bring with you for last-minute reference. Remember, if you do not follow the schedule, even an outstanding bloom will be disqualified.

Extra Water—Carry a thermos or canteen of water to refill any partially empty tubes and whatever new containers you may use at the show.

Hypodermic Syringe or Baster—A narrow-point baster or hypodermic syringe, sold as an oil applicator for delicate machinery, is useful for filling small containers with water. The tiny bud vases often used for miniatures just cannot be filled except by inserting a small tube or pointed spout. Slightly larger containers can be filled with a turkey baster, one of my favorite tools for pot-watering tiny plants and seedlings, but also useful at the show table.

Arrangements of miniatures give us the pleasure of enjoying the flowers close by. Here I include 'Seabreeze' *(top right)*, 'Swedish Doll', *(center)*, 'Beauty Secret' *(right)*, 'Popcorn' and 'Simplex' *(left center)*, and some unnamed seedlings.

Moist Rags or Towelettes—These moist cleaners are handy for last-minute washing of foliage and stems.

Small Scissors—To cut away any damaged foliage or to recut stems if water stops rising.

Rubber Blower—A sturdy rubber air blower, sometimes sold as a teflon-tipped solder blower, is useful for pushing away dust or spilled pollen without actually touching flowers. You might also like this device as a mini baster, to fill containers with water; but use a second blower for this in order to keep one dry and one wet.

Entry Tags—Each show has official entry tags or forms that you must fill out correctly. Have some extras on hand. Double-check that you have the correct tags. Shows may have different color tags to designate entry categories, usually divided according to experience, such as novice,

Dried mini rose flowers are prepared in silica gel powder, then molded into clear plastic for jewelry.

This mini rose pendant was created by Mrs. John Ewing.

junior, and advanced. The entry clerk, or similar show official, will answer your questions and assist you in following the show rules.

Extra Containers—Some rose shows provide containers for all rose displays, while other shows provide only containers for single stems, and all arrangements must be in your own containers. See local show schedule for details.

19
Sources for
Plants and Supplies

You will find the most up-to-date offering of rose supplies and plants in the ads that run in *American Rose* magazine. Supplies especially designed for hybridizers are sometimes offered through the Rose Hybridizer's Association. Membership information about these important groups is outlined in chapter 18. The current address for each is:

> The American Rose Society
> P.O. Box 30,000
> Shreveport, Louisiana   71130

> The Rose Hybridizer's Association
> c/o Don B. Nielson, Membership Chairman
> 508 South Juniper
> Toppenish, Washington   98948

BUYING YOUR MINIATURE ROSES

For more than twenty years miniature roses have come into my garden from many sources. Some sad little twigs were received as free premiums, a few sturdy shrublets came from Jackson and Perkins when they first offered miniatures created by Dr. Morey, and numerous healthy new miniatures have come to me through the mails from around the United States. A few miniatures were purchased at local garden centers which in turn had obtained the plants from commercial wholesale nurseries. Still

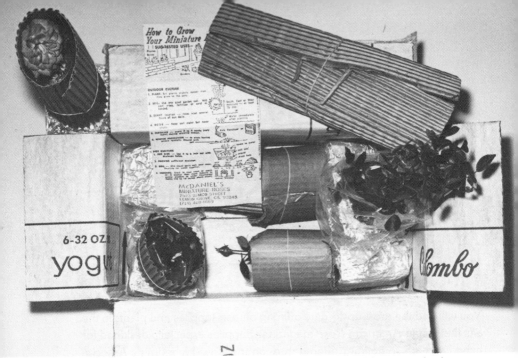

McDaniel's Miniature Rose Nursery in Lemon Grove, California, packs their rose shipments with a combination of aluminum, plastic bags, and cardboard protectors to surround the small plastic pots in which the roses are grown.

other miniatures were born here at Talisman Cove, growing from seed to flower under my own hand.

You will obtain the best roses, backed by a grower's personal guarantee, if you order by mail from miniature rose specialists. Even more exciting is to visit a miniature rose nursery and select the hybrids you like while the little plants are in bloom.

By visiting a nursery you can double-check that you like the colors, plant habit, and health of each bush. Some of the larger garden centers and a few specialists in unusual houseplants also carry miniature roses, but only as a sideline to their general stock. The nurseries that *only* deal in miniature roses will offer you the largest selection, sometimes more than two hundred different hybrids!

WHAT YOU SHOULD GET

Your new miniature roses should have sturdy, extensive root systems. Bushes must be free from pests. Check to be sure no free insects have been included as a bonus with your order. Miniature roses are shipped all twelve months of the year.

Chip Saville at Nor' East Miniature Roses personally inspects and grooms mini roses sent to customers.

Each shipment from Nor' East contains a helpful folder with basic culture notes. Bushes are grown and shipped in small plastic pots, individually packed in plastic bags and newspaper.

Some growers offer both growing, fully leafed-out plants and dormant bushes from cold storage or cool greenhouses. If you are ordering roses in the fall or winter to grow them indoors, it is an advantage to obtain dormant bushes. These have already had a cool rest period and are ready to start growing under your local conditions.

Dormant mini roses potted and then placed in good light (sun or fluorescents) will typically produce their first flush of blooms in 6 weeks. At warmer temperatures they flower somewhat faster, while with cool conditions growth and flowering will be slower.

This 'White Gem' bush was received during the winter from Star Roses. It soon began new growth when placed under fluorescent lights in average room temperatures.

Color descriptions in catalogs or the A.R.S. classifications will not always match the roses in your garden. Even when an official color chart such as this Nickerson color fan of Munsell hues is used to describe flower color, the flower hue varies according to culture and temperature.

TRANSITION

If you receive growing miniatures in full leaf, they are typically sent with flower buds ready to open or stems that will soon form buds. This is the type of bush you receive when ordering roses for shipment in late spring through early fall. But such active specimens may lose some foliage due to the shock of moving from one growing environment to another.

Plants grown under humid greenhouse conditions receive a shock if transferred directly to the garden or home. Roses grown outdoors in bright sun but then transferred to an indoor environment also must make a rather substantial adjustment. One way a plant adjusts to the transition is to lose leaves and slow growth. Already formed buds may blast or drop. If you are dealing with a well-grown, sturdy plant, there is no need to worry. The rose will make the transition in several weeks and then begin new growth that will be adapted to the new environment. It is a help to greenhouse-grown roses if you provide partial shade the first few days they are in the garden. If greenhouse-grown bushes are transferred to a windowsill or light garden, they will adjust more easily if humidity is 60 percent or more.

319

If you receive growing plants that need repotting at once, then mist the newly potted plants every morning. This added moisture sustains the bush until new feeder roots become established in the larger container.

ROOT BALLS

Some growers ship with rose root balls wrapped in moss, then aluminum foil. These plants must, of course, be repotted at once. Cut off any branches that have been broken in shipment and trim any damaged roots. If the bush has no broken parts, then do not trim or prune, just pot.

These sturdy bushes were sent to me from the Texas Mini Roses Nursery of Ernest Williams. Thanks to careful packing in moist sphagnum moss, aluminum foil, and plastic, they were received in perfect condition.

Still another shipping method is used by Star Roses, which mail potted mini roses wrapped in foil, then newspaper, and finally an outer protector of molded plastic. Star Roses also include a free culture folder.

Thousands of miniature roses are grown by Star Roses in West Grove, Pennsylvania, under thin plastic mesh during the summer.

Propagations of 'Starina' at Star Roses are grown in pots sunk into moist sand. This famous Meilland miniature is one of many European hybrids offered in the Conard-Pyle Star Roses catalog.

Other growers ship their plants in lightweight plastic pots, usually 3¼ inches deep by 2¾ inches across the top. Mini roses grown on benches where roots have a minimum opportunity to develop outside of the pot will make the smoothest transition. Some growers sink the mini rose pots into moist sand, which permits an extensive root system to develop *outside* of the pot once roots escape through drainage holes. When these bushes are shipped, the exterior roots are cut away. This causes some trauma to the bush, especially if a proportionate top section is not pruned.

If you receive a rose that shows heavy roots freshly trimmed but no top branches cut off, you should trim back the top at least ⅓ of the way, then repot the bush or plant in the garden. When root balls are very tightly ingrown, gently break apart the bottom 2 inches of roots to encourage new roots to grow out of the pot-bound mass.

The average mini rose shipped by the breeders who specialize in these plants will look like the bush in my potting photos in chapter 12. These sturdy, well-grown roses will cause you no trouble at all. In good soil, with reasonable care, they will quickly adjust and begin thanking you with wave after wave of delightful flowers.

Sequoia Nursery in California will prepare these bushes for mailing by removing plants from pots, wrapping the roots in aluminum foil, then newspaper. You can order mini roses any time of the year and receive them in good condition.

SUPPLIERS

Here is a list of reliable firms that can supply plants and growing supplies.

Company	Offerings
Abbey Garden 176 Toro Canyon Road Carpinteria, California 93013	Illustrated catalog (25¢) includes many unusual succulents suitable for growing with roses
Armstrong Nurseries Inc. Ontario, California 91761	Free catalog features larger roses, but this firm has been breeding miniatures and will soon release some new hybrids plus those from other hybridizers
Bio-Control Co. 10180 Ladybird Drive Auburn, California 95603	Live ladybugs, praying mantis egg cases; free leaflets

Company	*Offerings*
Brookstone Co. Peterborough, New Hampshire 03458	Free illustrated catalog lists useful tools for gardening
W. Atlee Burpee Co. Warminster, Pennsylvania 18974	Free color catalog includes some mini roses, many growing supplies, companion plants
P. de Jager & Sons Inc. South Hamilton, Massachusetts 01982	Free catalog of bulbs, including many miniature types
DG Shelter Products Vita Bark Division 401 Watt Avenue Sacramento, California 95825	Potting soils and mulch; free folder on product uses
Encap Products Co. P.O. Box 278 Mount Prospect, Illinois 60056	Green Garde iron
Floralite Co. 4124 East Oakwood Road Oak Creek, Wisconsin 53154	Useful catalog of indoor light fixtures, stands, water sprayers; free lists
Arthur Freed Orchids Inc. 5731 South Bonsall Drive Malibu, California 90265	Outstanding new Phalaenopsis orchids suitable as companions for indoor mini roses; free catalog
The Green House 9515 Flower Street Bellflower, California 90706	Gro-Cart indoor light stands; free brochure
Gurney Seed and Nursery Co. Yankton, South Dakota 57078	Free catalog offers a few mini roses, many growing supplies
HHH Horticultural 68 Brooktree Road Hightstown, New Jersey 08520	Hardiness zone maps, plant finders lists, vast selection of books; free catalog

Company	Offerings
Jackson and Perkins Medford, Oregon 97501	Free catalog of standard roses and growing supplies; sometimes offers minis in gift sets
Jones and Scully 2200 Northwest 33rd Avenue Miami, Florida 33142	Outstanding color illustrated catalog ($3.00) lists orchids and many growing supplies
Kartuz Greenhouses 92 Chestnut Street Wilmington, Massachusetts 01887	Catalog (50¢) offers many indoor plants, some suitable as rose companions
Logee's Greenhouses Danielson, Connecticut 06239	Catalog ($1.00) offers many miniature geraniums, begonias, and other indoor plants
Lord and Burnham Co. Irvington, New York 10533	Free greenhouse catalog lists some growing supplies, too
Lyndon Lyon Dolgeville, New York 13329	Free catalog (send 13¢ stamp); many gesneriads, some new mini roses
McDaniel's Miniature Roses 7523 Zemco Street Lemon Grove, California 92045	Free catalog of miniature roses, many hybrids, new and old
Marko Co. 94 Porete Avenue North Arlington, New Jersey 07032	Unusual indoor light fixtures with wedged louvers to stop glare; free folder
Mellinger's 2310 West South Range Road North Lima, Ohio 44452	Free catalog lists growing supplies, light fixtures, pots, etc.
Merry Gardens Camden, Maine 04843	Illustrated booklet ($1.00) and current catalog (25¢) list many unusual houseplants
Miniature Plant Kingdom 4125 Harrison Grade Road Sebastopol, California 95472	Free catalog lists over 200 different mini roses

Company	*Offerings*
Mini Roses Box 4255 Dallas, Texas 75208	Free catalog of hybridizer Ernest Williams lists many modern miniatures, new creations
Nor' East Miniature Roses 58 Hammond Street Rowley, Massachusetts 01969	Free catalog from hybridizer Harm Saville has extensive listings, color illustrations, helpful descriptions
Oakhill Gardens Route 3, Box 87 Dallas, Oregon 97338	Specialists in sempervivums and unusual sedums; list, 25¢
Oregon Bulb Farms P.O. Box 529 Gresham, Oregon 97030	Breeders of world famous lilies; color catalog, $1.00
Geo. W. Park Seed Co. P.O. Box 31 Greenwood, South Carolina 29647	Free catalog includes seed of miniature roses, light fixtures, growing supplies, companion plants
Pixie Treasures Mini Roses 4121 Prospect Avenue Yorba Linda, California 92686	Free illustrated catalog with many miniature hybrids; display garden for visitors
Sequoia Nursery 2519 East Noble Avenue Visalia, California 93277	Free folders and color illustrated catalog from hybridizer Ralph Moore list the best in modern miniature roses; also mini rose trees
Shoplite Co. 566 Franklin Avenue Nutley, New Jersey 07110	Complete catalog (25¢) of indoor light growing fixtures, tubes, plant stands
Star Roses Conard-Pyle Co. West Grove, Pennsylvania 19390	Free color illustrated catalog includes miniatures from European hybridizers, many larger roses, growing supplies
Texas Greenhouse Co. 2717 St. Louis Avenue Fort Worth, Texas 76110	Free catalog lists greenhouses and greenhouse supplies

Company	*Offerings*
Thompson and Morgan Inc. P.O. Box 24 Somerdale, New Jersey 08083	Free color illustrated catalog of unusual companion plants, some growing supplies
Tillotson's Roses 802 Brown's Valley Road Watsonville, California 95076	Specialists in old-fashioned roses, some of which are in background of miniatures; charming informative catalog ($1.00)
Tube Craft Inc. 1311 West 80th Street Cleveland, Ohio 44102	Free folder shows sturdy Flora Cart light stands and related indoor light-garden supplies
Uncle Charlie's Rose Products Rural Route No. 1 Finchville, Kentucky 40022	Free listing of rose growing supplies includes fertilizers and various sprays
White Flower Farm Litchfield, Connecticut 06759	Fine selection of outdoor companions including unusual heathers and heaths; illustrated catalog subscription, $4.00 for two editions
Melvin E. Wyant Rose Specialist Inc. Johnny Cake Ridge Mentor, Ohio 44060	Free list of miniature and larger roses

Bibliography

The American Rose Society. *The American Rose*. Shreveport, La. (periodical).

_____. *American Rose Annual*. The American Rose Society, The International Registration Authority for Roses.

_____. *Modern Roses 7*. Harrisburg, Pa.: The McFarland Company, 1969.

Ortho Books Editorial Staff. *Gardening Shortcuts*. San Francisco, Ca.: Ortho Books, 1974.

Pinney, Margaret E. *The Miniature Rose Book*. Princeton, N.J.: D. Van Nostrand Company, Inc., 1964.

Westcott, Cynthia. *Anyone Can Grow Roses*. New York: D. Van Nostrand Company, Inc., 1965. (Collier Books ed., 1967).

Young, Norman. *The Complete Rosarian*. Edited by L. A. Wyatt. New York: St. Martin's Press. 1971.

Index

Note: Italic page numbers indicate art.